P9-DZA-039

Morality

Publication of the paperback edition of
Morality: The Catholic View
was aided in part by a grant from the
Strake Foundation.

Morality
The Catholic View

Servais Pinckaers, O.P.

Preface by
Alasdair MacIntyre

Translated by
Michael Sherwin, O.P.

ST. AUGUSTINE'S PRESS
South Bend, Indiana

Translation copyright © 2001 by St. Augustine's Press

Original French edition of *La morale catholique*
Copyright © 1991 by Les edition du Cerf

All rights reserved. No part of this book may be reproduced, stored in a retrieval system, or transmitted, in any form or by any means, electronic, mechanical, photocopying, recording, or otherwise, without the prior permission of St. Augustine's Press.

Manufactured in the United States of America.

6 7 8   23 22

Library of Congress Cataloging in Publication Data
Pinckaers, Servais.
    [Morale catholique. English]
    Morality : the Catholic view / Servais Pinckaers ; preface by Alasdair MacIntyre; translated by Michael Sherwin.
        p.   cm.
    Includes bibliographical references and indexes.
    ISBN 1-58731-515-7 (pbk.: alk. paper)
    1. Christian ethics – Catholic authors. I. Title.
BJ1249 .P5513 2003
241'.042 – dc21   2002151652

Nihil obstat: Michael Heintz
Imprimatur: John M. D'Arcy
June 11, 2000

The nihil obstat *and* imprimatur *are offiical declarations that a book or pamphlet is free of doctrinal or moral error. No implication is contained therein that those who have granted the* nihil obstat *and* imprimatur *agree with the contents, opinions, or statements expressed.*

∞ *The paper used in this publication meets the minimum requirements of the American National Standard for Information Sciences – Permanence of Paper for Printed Materals, ANSI Z39.48–1984.*

ST. AUGUSTINE'S PRESS
www.staugustine.net

Table of Contents

Preface

Father Servais Pinckaers, O.P., is an extraordinary author, and this is an extraordinary book. The extraordinariness lies in Father Pinckaers' rare ability to know precisely what needs to be said and when and how and to whom to say it. In 1985 he published *Les sources de la morale chrétienne*, not only a timely book, but also the single most striking exposition of the ethics of Christianity for a long time. In it he shed new light on the controversies of the preceding forty years within Catholic communities and provided an alternative way of understanding Christian ethics that overcame the misunderstandings of those controversies. This he achieved in part by identifying what it is that makes a Christian perspective on the moral life distinctive and in part by exhibiting the different parts played in its formation and formulations by the gospels, the Pauline episteles, the Fathers, St. Thomas, and the later scholastics and manualists.

What Father Pinckaers made clear to us was the irrelevance of those preceding debates of recent years, debates that had been informed by false choices between inadequately characterized alternatives: Is the moral life about rules or consequences? Which has priority, authority or autonomy? Is our language to be scholastic or patristic? Should we make use neither of the scholastics nor the Fathers, but return to the New Testament? Are we to look to the Second Vatican Council or to its predecessors? What Father Pinckaers provided was a historical perspective in which later Christian writers, whether patristic or scholastic or modern, are understood as contributing to and enriching our reading of scripture. The culmination of his argument is a wonderfully illuminating enquiry into the relationship of human freedom to the natural law.

That earlier book was primarily for Catholic teachers, for the theologically and philosophically educated, and it offered its analysis in a manner appropriate to that audience. Now in *Morality: The Catholic View* (originally *La morale catholique*) Father Pinckaers has written a book that condenses the insights of his earlier work and presents them in a manner accessible to the general reader. Just as the earlier book was well designed to meet the needs of teachers of theology, this new work is well designed to meet the needs of their students. Yet this is a timely book not only for Catholic students, but also for anyone wishing to engage with the Catholic view of the moral life. This book will speak to Catholic and non-Catholic Christians alike, and even to non-Christians, opening up dialogue and enriching our shared enquiries. And it is a book that will challenge and inform all of us, teachers and students alike.

Les sources de la morale chrétienne was published in English in an excellent translation as *The Sources of Christian Ethics* (Washington, D.C.: Catholic University of America Press, 1995). The translation of *Morality: The Catholic View* by Father Michael Sherwin, O.P., is equally impressive and we are very much in his debt. It is my hope and prayer that this book will be read widely in English-speaking countries.

March, 2000
Alasdair MacIntyre

Introduction

Catholic moral teaching is not a mere code of prescriptions and prohibitions. It is not something that the Church teaches merely to keep people obedient, doing violence to their freedom. Rather, Catholic morality is a response to the aspirations of the human heart for truth and goodness. As such, it offers guidelines that when followed will make these aspirations grow and become strong under the warm light of the Gospel. Catholic morality is not by nature oppressive; nor is it in principle conservative. It seeks to educate for growth. This is its true mission.

Catholic moral teaching is not reserved solely to the faithful of the Roman Church, but reaches out to all the world in two fundamental ways. First, it seeks to interpret the natural law inscribed in every human heart, taking the Ten Commandments as a starting point. Second, because its source is the Gospel, Catholic moral teaching also participates in the universal dynamism that the Spirit confers upon the Word of Christ.

Stability and Change in Moral Teaching

The task of moral theologians is complex; their task is to respond continually, as a work of education, to the questions posed to them. Catholic moral teaching has exhibited great stability over the course of history, both in the teaching of precepts and in their application. It has been

1

compared to a rock that remains firm in the midst of fluc-
tuations of thought and practice. Christians, however,
have not been satisfied merely to observe and transmit
rules of behavior. Searching to understand the teachings
they have received, and confronted with the philosophies
and cultures of their day, they have endeavored to present,
explain, and systematize the evangelical doctrine in order
to make it more understandable to others, and when
needed to defend its message against attacks and to support its missionary vigor. Moral theology is born of this
Christian reflection and in turn nourishes the Church's
preaching and catechesis.

Working in and through the cultures of each age, this
reflection has produced numerous works of great variety,
each of which is grafted onto a common moral teaching
under the auspices of the ecclesial Magisterium. The
Christian heritage is richer and more diverse than one
often thinks. It forms a type of cultural memory upon
which we all depend, even without our knowing it. To a
large extent it determines our way of approaching moral
problems. Therefore, even a brief summary of the moral
concepts that have been developed in the Church can
prove helpful, especially in this time when the very foundations of morality are shaken and frequently called into
question among theologian and layperson alike.

An Effort at Renewal
The Second Vatican Council recognized that the manuals
used for teaching moral theology over the course of recent
centuries suffered from certain limitations and deficien-
cies. The Council mandated an effort of renewal. It asked
that moral theology exhibit three central traits. First the
Council asked that moral theology be more deeply nourished by the teachings of the Scriptures and the Fathers of
the Church. Second, it asked that moral theology be linked

more successfully to dogmatic theology and to the doctrines of the Trinity, Christ, and the sacraments. Third, the Council asked that moral theology be grounded more adequately both scientifically and philosophically, in order to ensure a more judicious engagement with contemporary thought (*Decree on the Training of Priests*, n. 16). These requests are in harmony with the aspirations of many Christians. Having discovered the Bible and the liturgy anew, they seek a moral theology more deeply rooted in these sources. Better informed of their responsibilities in the world, they seek to face the new ethical problems posed by the sciences and technology.

Our Plan and Its Limits
This book proceeds from within this dual scriptural and philosophical perspective. It is divided into two parts. The first presents the sources of Christian moral teaching and the principal stages of its theological development. The second offers a synthetic presentation of Catholic moral teaching that strives to be faithful to its origins and true to the requirements of renewal.

"Catholic" Moral Teaching
There is one last clarification we should make. The subject of this book is moral theology as it has been taught by the Catholic Church through the centuries. Thus, we shall not treat directly Protestant ethics nor the moral teaching of the Orthodox Church. Nevertheless, we use the term "catholic" in the broad sense. Because of its primitive sources, including Jewish sources, and because of a long common history, Catholic moral theology is closely related to the moral theologies of other confessions. It can, therefore, be of interest to all Christians and to all people who engage in ethical reflection.

Part I

A Richer History than One Might Think

I

The Gospel Sources

Ancient Moral Catechesis

The New Testament contains numerous moral texts, both in the words of the Lord as reported by the evangelists and in the apostolic preaching. This teaching has its roots in the Old Testament, but deepens its doctrine and imparts a new dimension by placing it in relation to the person and life of Jesus.

The apostles and the first Christian communities took particular care to compile and transmit a precise moral catechesis faithful to the teaching of their Lord. The most representative example is the Sermon on the Mount. It gathers together in one great discourse, after the manner of the historians of antiquity, the teachings of Christ that present the rules of life, rules that will enable his disciples to attain a "justice surpassing that of the scribes and Pharisees."

In order, however, to appreciate adequately the ethical character of these texts, we must remove from our minds certain modern notions that inhibit our ability to interpret them correctly. Moral theology has become the domain of obligations and legal imperatives and has set aside the question of happiness or perfection. Hence, it especially separates itself from spirituality and from *parenesis*, which is a form of exhortation. Such divisions were unknown in antiquity; one cannot apply them to the writings of the New Testament without being anachronistic. These divisions have led many interpreters, theologians, and

7

exegetes to view the scriptural texts that go beyond the level of strict obligations as not properly belonging to moral theology; this explains why these texts generally attract so little attention. This mindset is a major intellectual obstacle inhibiting our return to the ancient sources of the Christian life.

The Gospel texts presuppose a different conception of the moral life. Their moral teaching is a response to the question of happiness and of salvation. It offers a description of the ways of wisdom that lead to holiness and perfection through living the virtues and the precepts. From this perspective, moral theology encompasses a larger domain. It recovers the sapiential and spiritual dimensions essential to it. The Sermon on the Mount, for example, responds directly to the moral question understood in this way. It begins by announcing the Beatitudes; it then extends the moral pathways traced in the Ten Commandments to the precept: "be perfect, as your heavenly Father is perfect."

The Sermon on the Mount

Let us review rapidly the principal passages of the New Testament that offer moral catechesis, focusing above all on two characteristic texts. The Sermon on the Mount stands out at once. It is the first of five discourses that are the linchpins of Matthew's Gospel. It assembles the essential elements of Jesus' teaching on justice and the moral rules offered to his disciples. It is an explanation of the call to conversion: "Repent, for the kingdom of heaven is at hand" (*Mt* 4.17).

This discourse, which draws together into an ordered whole words that might well have been spoken on different occasions, is a model of the ancient moral catechesis. It can justly be called a "charter of the Christian life." The Sermon enjoys the authority of the Lord, expressed in

8

categorical formulas: "Unless your justice surpass that of the scribes and Pharisees, you will not enter the kingdom of heaven"; "you have heard it said. . . . But I say to you. . . ." The text has undergone a work of redaction that has not been sufficiently recognized. It is composed of short phrases, often arranged together to form compact units such as the Beatitudes. They are bundles of condensed doctrine fashioned for oral transmission as well as for meditation. Assembled together they form a body of doctrine inspired by a single guiding wisdom. The Sermon is not a mosaic of disparate sayings. Although it does not follow the logic of abstract reason, it does exhibit an underlying unity. It conforms to the often contrasting movements of the deep intelligence of the human heart revealed in human experience. As John Chrysostom and Augustine well understood and explained to their people, the Sermon is addressed to all, beginning with the poor and the afflicted. Thus, contrary to what will too often be claimed later, it is not reserved to a religious elite.

The *structure of the Sermon* in its broad outline is relatively simple.

1. The Beatitudes take up the promises made to the Chosen People since the time of Abraham. These are the numerous blessings scattered throughout the Scriptures, as for example in the first verses of the Psalter. The Beatitudes focus the hope of the disciples upon the kingdom of heaven, paradoxically directed to the poor and those persecuted for Jesus' sake, a message that expresses the experience of the first Christian generations. The Fathers saw in the Beatitudes the response of Christ to the question of happiness. When they present Jesus as addressing the philosophers' central question, the question of happiness, they are portraying him as the true sage.

2. After the description of the disciples as the "salt of the earth" and "the light of the world," there is the

description of the "justice" of the moral law according to Christ. This description develops five of the precepts of the Ten Commandments by means of contrast: "You have heard it said. . . . But I say to you. . . ." Justice is henceforth placed at the level of the human heart, at the roots of action. It is there that the love of God and neighbor is formed and attains its summit in the forgiveness of one's enemies, imitating the mercy and perfection of the heavenly Father.

3. Next there is the reordering of three primary acts of a pious life: almsgiving (the archetypical form of mutual assistance), prayer, and fasting (the principal form of asceticism). Instead of doing these acts to be seen by one's fellows, one should engage in them for love of the Father who sees in secret. We return once again to the level of the heart's intention, which places us by faith and love in communion with the Father. It is here at this central point in the Sermon that Matthew inserts the *Our Father*.

4. The last section is more diverse and brings together sayings that invite us to seek our true treasure in heaven. We are to guard against the attraction of wealth and to be benevolent in our judgments. We are also called to persevere confidently in our prayer.

5. The conclusion of the Sermon summarizes the teaching of the Law: It presents the Golden Rule as a practical criterion of discernment; it offers us a choice between the narrow way that leads to life and the broad way that leads to perdition; it distinguishes false prophets from true disciples by noting whether they practice the Word and exhibit the fruits and perseverance that the Word produces. The evangelist notes in conclusion the admiration of the crowd before the authority of Jesus, an authority that he will subsequently reveal through a series of healings.

The modern interpretation of the Sermon on the Mount has principally addressed the issue of whether one can put this teaching into practice. The difficulty of interpreting the Sermon has been increased by the habit of viewing the Law as a code of obligations. In reality, the Sermon describes the ways of the kingdom of heaven toward which the Holy Spirit wishes to lead the disciples by faith in Jesus, a faith that operates through charity. Thus, the Sermon is integrated into a Gospel that both announces "Jesus Christ the Son of God," and calls us to believe in him. This response of faith is impossible for those who count only on their own strength. The Sermon on the Mount, however, describes itself as accessible to the humblest who know how to receive the gift of grace and love. This, at least, is how the Fathers interpret the Sermon.

The "Paraclesis" of the Letter to the Romans

We find the second example of moral teaching in the second part of the letter to the *Romans*, in chapters 12 to 15. It is a model of apostolic catechesis. It has a different style from the Sermon: While the Sermon enjoys the authority of the Lord whose words it proclaims in formulations, the letter to the *Romans* presents the doctrine of an apostle who shares what he himself has received. The passage begins with a significant term, a term that reappears regularly in St. Paul: "I exhort you brothers and sisters. . . ." The moral teaching of the apostles is made in the manner of an exhortation among brothers and sisters in the name of the Lord from whom it receives its force. We shall call this mode of teaching a "*paraclesis*" (from the Greek word that Paul employs: *parakaleo* [I exhort], from which comes "Paraclete," a word signifying the Holy Spirit [*Jn* 14.26]). We do so in preference to the usual "*parenesis*," since *parenesis* evokes a simple recommendation on the spiritual plane, without any direct impact in moral science. This great text from *Romans* was continually commented on by the Fathers and the early scholastics. Yet, like the Sermon on the Mount, it was much neglected in the years that followed.

The *paraclesis* of the letter to the *Romans* depends directly on the first part of the letter, which deals with justification by faith, life in the Spirit, and the love of Christ. The *paraclesis* explains concretely how those who believe in Jesus and are animated by his Spirit are called to live. This progression is natural and would not have caused difficulty if later theologians had not intervened to cut the thread that joins the two halves of the letter. Among Catholics this separation was expressed in the division between dogmatic theology, to which the teaching of faith belongs, and moral theology, to which the second part of the letter was relegated, and subsequently reduced to a form of spiritual exhortation. Among Protestants the opposition was between faith, which alone justifies (a topic treated at the beginning of the letter) and works, along with the virtues (a topic addressed in the second part of the letter).

In our view, it is not possible to return to the apostolic sources unless we discover how to reestablish the connection between the act of faith and the moral life, and thereby recover the holistic unity of *Romans*.

The *paraclesis* of chapters 12 to 15 possesses a specific structure and sketches for us the dominant lines of Gospel morality, coming to a close by offering a response to certain precise problems. The stages of this teaching are the following.

1. The Christian life is true worship. It is a liturgy where we offer to God as a living sacrifice our bodies and our persons, discerning what is good and pleasing to him. The term "body" (*soma*) employed here evokes the body of

Christ offered in the Eucharist and the body that forms the Church (12.1–2). One can, therefore, refer to the liturgical dimension of Christian morality.

2. Shaped by faith, moral teaching takes place within the context of the faithful's participation in the body of Christ. They are members of this body and have received a multitude of gifts and ministries that they exercise for the good of all (vv. 3–8). This is the ecclesial dimension of the apostolic moral teaching, which returns to the fore in *1 Corinthians* (ch. 12).

3. This ecclesial unity and generosity are the work of charity. Paul describes charity through a collection of characteristics that form a prototypical passage composed of brief, well-chosen notes that in Greek have an assonance and rhythm that facilitate memorization. With these successive brushstrokes, St. Paul paints for us the face of the Christian (vv. 9–13). (See C. H. Dodd, *Gospel and Law: The Relation of Faith and Ethics in Early Christianity* [Cambridge: Cambridge University Press, 1957]).

4. The picture is completed by a passage full of energy that calls to mind the Sermon on the Mount: the invitation to bless one's persecutors, to seek out what is humble, and to conquer evil with good. This is the summit of Gospel *agape* (vv. 14–21).

5. After this more general part, Paul presents the attitude that Christians should hold toward civil authority, which at that time was pagan. One should offer civil authority a frank and active obedience, an obedience that flows from one's submission to God and love of neighbor, which the Apostle sees as the summation of the entire Law (ch. 13.1–10).

6. Pauline moral teaching also has an eschatological dimension: sustained by the hope that the coming of Christ is a day that is going to appear, the Christian is invited to "put on Christ," and in the light of Christ to remain

vigilant in the battle against the works of darkness (vv. 11–14).

7. The Apostle next examines at length (chs. 14 to 15.6) the delicate problem of divergent practices among the faithful with regard to diet and days of the week. Paul's response is a model of Christian discernment in the treatment of cases of conscience, something that we also find

---

The Face of Charity

Romans 12.9–13

Let love be sincere; hate what is evil, hold fast to what is good; love one another with fraternal affection; anticipate one another in showing honor. Do not grow slack in zeal, be fervent in the Spirit, serve the Lord. Rejoice in hope, be patient in affliction, persevere in prayer. Contribute to the needs of the saints, practice hospitality.

1 Corinthians 13.4–7

Love is patient; love is kind. Love is not jealous; it is not boastful; it is not arrogant or rude; it does not seek its own interests; it is not quick-tempered; it does not brood over evil; it does not rejoice over wrongdoing but rejoices with the truth. Love bears all things, believes all things, hopes all things, endures all things.

Galatians 5.22–26

The fruit of the Spirit is love, joy, peace, patience, kindness, goodness, faithfulness, gentleness, self-control. Against such there is no law. Now those who belong to Christ Jesus have crucified their flesh with its passions and desires. If we live in the Spirit, let us also follow the Spirit. Let us not be conceited, provoking one another, envious of one another.

---

in *1 Corinthians*. St. Paul demonstrates with great refinement how to give priority to fraternal charity in the discussion of concrete cases.

8. The conclusion takes up again the major themes of the entire letter, offering the example of Christ. Christ became the servant of all (Jews and Pagans) in order that they might live as brothers and sisters in the faith through the mercy of God and the power of the Holy Spirit.

The Other Texts Containing Moral Teaching

Besides these prototypical examples of the moral catechesis of the apostolic period, we should note a series of other texts that are often equally rich. The order in which they appear in the Scriptures is as follows.

1 Corinthians: Paul first examines a series of "cases of conscience," concerning incest, recourse to pagan tribunals, fornication, and so forth, which he resolves through rational arguments and chiefly in reference to Christ (chs. 5–11). Paul then in chapters 12 and 13 presents the hierarchy of the Spirit's gifts. Principal among these gifts is charity, which holds the body of Christ (the Church) together and inspires the other virtues, ministries, and charisms.

Galatians 5: Paul offers a description of spiritual combat that opposes the works of the flesh against the fruits of the Spirit, beginning with charity.

Ephesians 4.1–5.32: an exhortation to preserve the unity of the one Body and the one Spirit by casting off the "old self" and putting on "the new self . . . created in God's way in justice and holiness of truth."

Philippians 2.1–17 and 3.1–4.9: an exhortation to imitate the attitude of Christ in humility and obedience to the cross in order to participate in his glory and to become imitators of Paul, who strains in his race to seize the prize that is knowledge of Jesus.

Colossians 3.1–4.6: an exhortation to love in Christ in order to put on the new self "which is being renewed in knowledge after the image of its creator." We note as well the two great introductory hymns of *Colossians* and *Ephesians* (*Col* 1.15–20 and *Eph* 1.3–14), which describe the mystery of salvation in Christ, offered as the object of Christian hope and contemplation; they reveal our destiny according to the divine plan.

1 Thessalonians 4.1–5.28: an exhortation to holiness and vigilance in waiting for the Day of the Lord. We are to wait as children of the light in the imitation of Christ, an imitation that underlies one's imitation of the Apostle and of one's brothers and sisters (*1 Thes* 1.6–8 and *2 Thes* 3.7).

Let us add several references to other New Testament writings that present a moral doctrine.

James, with its wise teaching, so concrete and pungent.

1 Peter, which is a veritable jewel of moral *paraclesis,* whose teaching is often close to that of Paul and the Sermon on the Mount.

1 John, with its great and characteristically Johannine themes: the light of the Word and the darkness; sin and the world, charity and faith.

Two Poles of the Moral Teaching of St. Paul

In conclusion let us turn to the two major poles of the moral teaching of St. Paul that will guide later theology.

1. In the face of Jewish moral teaching (which laid claim to justice) and Greek moral teaching (which alleged to have wisdom), and in light of their inadequacy, *Paul puts forward a moral teaching that has a new source: the person of Jesus* who shares with his disciples the justice and wisdom of God, through faith and the work of charity poured into their hearts by the action of the Holy Spirit. Christian action, therefore, is equally a life "in Christ," and a life "in

the Spirit." The trilogy of faith, hope, and charity control the other gifts and virtues.

2. At the same time, *Paul invokes the creative work of God in nature and in the conscience of the human person, in harmony with the Gospel.* Two texts stand out in this regard: according to *Romans* 1.19–20 and 2.26, the pagans can both know God by his works and know the moral law written in their hearts. Paul recommends to the Philippians that they have concern for "whatever is true, whatever is honorable, whatever is just . . . if there is any virtue and if there is anything worthy of praise" (*Phil* 4.8). This is an invitation to receive with discernment whatever is just and best in the teaching of the philosophers, even among the pagans; Paul himself does not hesitate to borrow at times from popular stoicism, and to offer reflections that appeal to human common sense in the judgment of cases of conscience. This double foundation, supplied by faith and by reason, grace and nature, will be taken up continuously in the teaching of subsequent generations, but the emphasis will vary greatly from one period of the Church's history to another.

Lastly, let us note a fundamental rule of interpretation for all of these evangelical texts: one cannot understand fully their moral teaching unless one puts it into practice in a spirit of faith. The interior experience of living these texts reveals their reality and truth, which can be compared to a rock on which one can build solidly. We are not dealing here merely with a collection of beautiful ideas, but with a Word that grounds existence and gives life to those who docilely and actively receive it.

II

The Moral Teaching of the Fathers of the Church

The Fathers of the Church merit their name: They truly built up the Church on the foundation laid by the Gospel in every area of the Christian life. Thus, their works are a privileged source for us. The Fathers especially excel in the art of making from the Scriptures a spiritual bread that is nourishing, pleasing to the palate, and still retains its freshness.

The principal characteristics of the Fathers' teaching are the following.

1. *The first and constant source of their doctrine is the Scriptures.* The Fathers center their teaching on the person and the work of Christ as presented in the Gospels, which bear their fruit from within the life of the Church: through the preaching of the bishop who comments on the Scriptures; through the celebration of the divine liturgy, which in prayer meditates on the Scriptures; and lastly through putting the Scriptures into practice, which renders them efficacious. The moral doctrine of the Fathers, therefore, is found principally in homilies that explain the Scriptures to the people, as is the case with St. Augustine and St. John Chrysostom. The Fathers also write works of their own devising to explain Christian moral teaching to the pagans, as for example, *The Pedagogue*, by Clement of Alexandria and the treatise *On the Morals of the Catholic Church*, by St. Augustine. There are, in addition, patristic works that address particular moral questions, such as

marriage and virginity, lying, patience, fasting, and so forth. St. Augustine wrote such works, but so did others, such as Tertullian and St. Cyprian.

2. The second characteristic of the teaching of the Fathers is its *judicious use of resources drawn from Greco-Roman culture and philosophy*. Having established the primacy of faith and the mystery of Christ presented by the Scriptures, the Fathers do not hesitate to employ what is true and good in the thought of their day. They draw upon the Stoics, such as Seneca and Cicero; they find resources among the Platonists, such as Plotinus in the case of St. Augustine; or, like St. John of Damascus, they turn to Aristotelian thought. They draw on pagan thought and culture in order to place it in the service of the Gospel. It is from this collaboration between faith and reason that theology is born. The Fathers especially take advantage of pagan moral teaching concerning the virtues, vices, and contemplation. They adopt the four classical cardinal virtues: prudence, justice, courage, and temperance, which are surrounded by numerous annexed virtues, and are already mentioned in *Wisdom* (8.7). This process of assimilation is made easier by the fact that the Fathers, like the philosophers, consider the moral life as a quest for happiness, and see in the practice of the virtues the best response to the primordial question of happiness posed by every human heart. Nevertheless, the inclusion of faith and charity modifies the classical perspective and even changes the conception of virtue, making it a gift from God, a grace rather than solely the work of unaided human effort.

3. Lastly, the moral teaching of the Fathers is *inseparable from the great spiritual currents animating the Church of their day*. The Fathers faithfully represent these currents: the spirituality of the martyrs, which dominated the first three

centuries of the Church and which touched the lives of Christians from every social strata; the ideal of virginity; monastic spirituality; and the quest for the wisdom that comes from the Holy Spirit. These spiritual movements, which form the lion's share of the moral teaching of the Fathers, maintained throughout the Church the vigor of the evangelical life. In no way, therefore, do the Fathers separate spirituality from morality. In their view, all Christians have been called to "live in the Spirit," according to the graces they have received and the diversity of the vocations to which they have been called.

Two Examples from St. Augustine

St. Augustine provides us two helpful examples of the attempt to present Christian morality. In his brief work, *On the Morals of the Catholic Church*, which is a response to the Manichees, Augustine poses the question of morality on the level of reason:

> How then, according to reason, ought humans to live? Everyone wants to be happy. Everyone will agree with me on this almost before the words are out of my mouth (3.4).

The first task, therefore, is to determine what good makes the human person happy. Augustine shows that the perfect good should be greater than humans themselves: The sovereign good is God. At this point, faith comes to the aid of reason and through its wisdom teaches reason the way to happiness. One may describe this way in a single phrase: to love God with all one's heart; it is the charity taught and inspired by Christ. Charity born of faith, therefore, will be the principal Christian virtue.

But what is charity's relationship to the human

virtues delineated by the philosophers? Augustine's solution to this question is original and profound: The cardinal virtues are simply four forms of charity. Prudence is love that discerns the useful good; justice is love that serves what it loves; courage is courageous love; temperance is love that gives itself completely to what it loves. In this way Augustine solidly establishes the connection between the theological and cardinal virtues, a connec-

As to whether virtue leads us to the happy life, I hold that virtue is nothing other than the perfect love of God. Now, when it is said that virtue has a fourfold division, as I understand it, this is said according to the various movements of love. Thus, these four virtues (would that all had the strength of these virtues in their minds as they have their names in their mouths!), I do not hesitate to define them as follows: temperance is love giving itself entirely to the beloved; courage is love readily bearing all things for the sake of the beloved; justice is love serving only the beloved and therefore ruling rightly; prudence is love distinguishing wisely between what hinders it and what helps it. But, as we have said, the object of this love is nothing other than God, the sovereign good, the highest wisdom and the perfect harmony. We may, therefore, define these virtues as follows: temperance is love preserving itself entire and incorrupt for God; courage is love readily bearing all things for the sake of God; justice is love serving only God, and therefore ruling well everything else that is subject to the human person; prudence is love discerning well between what helps it toward God and what hinders it.

St. Augustine
De moribus ecclesiae catholicae
15.25 (PL 32: 1322)

tion that will be the foundation for subsequent reflection on the structure of moral theology.

We note briefly a second original attempt by Augustine to express the morality of the Gospel. In his first homily on the Sermon on the Mount, a text that he views as gathering together all the precepts necessary for the Christian life, the Bishop of Hippo presents the Beatitudes as a description of the seven stages that lead the Christian toward the Kingdom of Heaven. The Christian life is a journey that begins in the humility of conversion and leads to purity of heart and peace in God. Augustine then places the Beatitudes in relation to the gifts of the Holy Spirit, as enumerated by the Prophet Isaiah in chapter 11 of the Septuagint version of the text. He does so both to demonstrate that we must have the grace of the Holy Spirit to advance along this path and to point out the form that grace takes on each stage of the journey. He completes his reflections by placing the seven petitions of the *Our Father* in relation to the Beatitudes and the gifts, for prayer is an indispensable means of obtaining the help of the Spirit. This theological construction, inspired by his meditation on the Scriptures and his own personal experience, especially as presented in his *Confessions*, will create a tradition of interpretation of the Sermon on the Mount that we can appropriately call a spirituality of the Beatitudes. This tradition of interpretation will be taken up by Thomas Aquinas in his *Summa theologiae*, who places it on the firm foundation offered by the seven principal virtues.

Conclusion

The Fathers of the Church, therefore, provide us with a moral view that is rich and varied. They offer a moral vision that is not only tied directly to the Gospel as read and lived by the Church, but which is also enriched by their reflection on the great human problems also treated

---

Fathers of the Church

Greek Fathers	Latin Fathers

Greek Fathers

Didache (c.100): the two ways, one which leads to life, the other to death.

St. Irenaeus (c.130–c.200): *Against the Heresies*: the configuring of the human person to the image of God and of Christ by the Holy Spirit.

Clement of Alexandria (c.150–c.211): *The Pedagogue*. Christ teaches the virtues.

Origen (c.185–c.255): *On First Principles*: freedom and the triumph of good. Commentaries on Scripture, and a treatise on prayer. Exhortation to martyrdom.

St. Athanasius (c.295–373): *The Life of St. Anthony of Egypt* (the Father of Western Monasticism).

St. Basil (330–379): *Morals*.

St. John Chrysostom (344–407): homilies on St. Matthew, St. John, St. Paul, and the *Psalms*. Moralist par excellence.

Pseudo-Dionysius the Areopagite (V to VI century): Master of mystical theology.

St. John of Damascus (c.675–749): concerning free action, the virtues, and the vices.

Latin Fathers

Tertullian (c.150–c.240): on the Roman games, on women's clothing, on chastity and monogamy, virgins, prayer, patience, and martyrdom.

St. Cyprian (c.210–258): on the theological virtues, prayer, virginity, martyrdom, and patience.

St. Ambrose (c.333–397): *On the Duties of the Clergy*: the linking of Scripture and Cicero in the presentation of Christian morality.

St. Augustine (354–430): philosophical dialogues, *On the Sermon on the Mount*, homilies on the *Gospel of John*, on *1 John*, on the *Psalms*, etc., *On the Morals of the Catholic Church*; *On Christian Doctrine*; *Enchiridion on Faith, Hope and Charity*; *The Confessions*; on lying, marriage, patience, etc. Writings on grace and free choice.

Pelagius (c.360–c.422): adversary of St. Augustine concerning freedom and grace, defender of the self-sufficiency of free choice for salvation.

St. Leo the Great (c.400–461): homilies on the principal feasts of the Christian life: a liturgical morality.

Boethius (480–525): *The Consolation of Philosophy*.

St. Gregory the Great (c.540–604): *On Pastoral Care, Moral Reflections on Job*, homilies on Ezekiel. Master of contemplation and the spiritual life.

by the philosophers. They probe the question of happiness in the face of suffering, sin, and death; they address the challenge of teaching the virtues, which they view as animated by faith and charity, as well as by the virtue of hope inspired by the divine promises. In this way, the Fathers regard Christ as the consummate man of wisdom, who provides the peoples of the world the true answers to their questions, answers rooted in the mystery of the cross and resurrection, and in the gift of the Spirit lived in the communion of all believers. The Fathers, it is true, do not systematize moral theology in the way that later generations will. Yet their moral teaching, because of its close proximity to the Scriptures and to the personal and ecclesial experience of Christians, as well as its close relationship to dogmatic theology and the liturgy, contains a fullness that makes it an inexhaustible heritage and a model to follow.

With respect to the years between the age of the Fathers and the thirteenth century, it will be helpful to point out the role played by the "penitentials" during the high Middle Ages. The "penitentials" were instruction manuals designed for confessors, which contained lists of sins and a corresponding table of penances to be imposed according to the type and gravity of the fault committed. These books are linked with the private practice of Penance. The penitentials emerge in the sixth century in the monasteries of Ireland and Britain, and subsequently spread to the continent. Their success will extend to the twelfth century. Their influence will subsequently be felt in the continued care taken to apply an appropriate penance to each sin, something one finds in more important works such as the *Summa theologiae moralis* of St. Antoninus of Florence (1389–1459) and in the pastoral works of St. Charles Borromeo (1538–1584). (See Pierre Michaud-Quantin, *Sommes de casuistique et manuels de confession au moyen-age* [Louvain: Nauwelaerts, 1962].)

III

The Classic Period of Western Theology

Saint Thomas Aquinas: The Morality of Happiness and the Virtues

The thirteenth century is the classical period of western theology. This period of theology coincides with the formation of independent townships and the birth of an urban mercantile class, as well as with the creation of universities and the construction of the gothic cathedrals. It also coincides with the spiritual movements initiated by St. Francis and St. Dominic and expressed in religious orders of a new type, different from the monks. It is the period when modern nations begin to form within the framework of a still united Europe.

Theology experiences a renewal following the discovery of the works of Aristotle and the introduction of the scholastic method. The scholastic method joins the reading of the Scriptures and of prestigious authors – the "authorities" as they were called – with the exercise of rational dialectic. This dialectic pits conflicting opinions against one other in an effort to arrive at the truth and to advance the frontiers of scientific knowledge in all domains. During this period, theology still maintains close ties with philosophy, law, and the other sciences within the structure of the newly emerging universities, especially at the University of Paris where St. Albert and St. Thomas taught.

It is the age of the "doctors" and of the "*summae*," works that present a synthesis of knowledge. Several

Since, as John of Damascus states, when we say that the human person is made in the image of God, image signifies the power intellectually and through free choice to move oneself, after treating the exemplar, namely God, and the things that flow from the divine power according to his will, it now remains for us to consider his image, namely man, as one who is the principle of his actions, having free choice and dominion over his works.

St. Thomas Aquinas
Summa theologiae (ST), Prologue to the *Secunda pars*

It is impossible for human happiness to consist in any created good. For happiness is the perfect good, which completely quiets the appetite: otherwise it would not be the last end, if something still remained to be desired. Now the object of the will (i.e., the object of the human appetite) is the universal good, just as the object of the intellect is the universal true. Hence it is evident that nothing can quiet the human will, except the universal good. This is found, not in anything created, but in God alone: because every creature has goodness by participation. Thus, God alone can satisfy the will of the human person, as is said in Psalm 103.5: "Who satisfies your desire with good things." In God alone, therefore, does human happiness consist.

ST I-II 2.8

names stand out: Alexander of Hales (1180–1245), St. Bonaventure (1221–1274), and Duns Scotus (c. 1264–1274) among the Franciscans; St. Albert the Great (1193–1280) and St. Thomas Aquinas (1225–1274) among the Dominicans. We shall give special attention to the work of St. Thomas. His moral teaching is particularly significant and fruitful, especially as he presents it in his *Summa theologiae*.

The plan St. Thomas follows in the *Summa theologiae* is comparable in its structure to the ordered columns in the nave of a cathedral. God made humans in his image by giving them mastery over their actions in the gift of freedom. As a result, moral theology, which establishes the rules for human action, takes its place between the first and the third parts of the *Summa*: between the first part of theology, which studies God – Father, Son and Holy Spirit (as well as the works of creation and Providence, unique among which is the human person with his natural desire to see God and his sins) – and the third part of the *Summa*, which treats Christ as our redeemer from sin and our way to return to God through the grace given by the sacraments.

Two Parts of Morality in the *Summa theologiae*

General (denoted internal and external)

Aquinas divides his presentation of morality into two parts, one general, the other particular. In the general part, the first question is the question of *happiness*, which dominates the whole of moral theology by establishing the ultimate end of life and of human action. Full happiness does not reside in wealth or glory or honors, or in knowledge or virtue, or in any created reality, but in the loving vision of God. After establishing the higher end of human life in this way, Aquinas analyzes the *voluntary act*, in its structure and in its moral quality. He next adds a remarkable and too-often-neglected study of the *passions* or emotions. Our acts have two types of principles, causes, or sources. Certain *principles* are *internal* or personal: These are the virtues or dynamic qualities of the spirit and the heart that are brought to perfection by the *gifts of the Holy Spirit*, along with the Beatitudes and the fruits of the Spirit. They also have contraries, which are the *vices* and *sins*.

27

Other principles of action have a source *external* to us: First, there is *law*, which is the work of a wisdom endowed with an impelling force. Law is multifaceted: The *eternal law* in God is inscribed in the heart of the human person as the natural law, which *human laws* apply and make more precise. Law is also expressed by revelation in the *Old Law* centered on the Ten Commandments and in the evangelical or *New Law*, which St. Thomas presents as an internal law: It is the grace itself of the Holy Spirit working in the human heart through faith in Christ and through charity. This *grace*, revealed in the Gospel and received through the sacraments, becomes a second principle of action, exterior in its origin, but profoundly interior through the depth of its penetration within us.

Particular (the virtues and the gifts)

The second or more particular part of moral theology is organized around the seven principal virtues that it considers. The analysis of each of these virtues includes a presentation of the opposing sins and the corresponding gifts of the Holy Spirit and precepts of the Ten Commandments. In the first place, there are the divine or *theological virtues: faith* and the corresponding gifts of intelligence and knowledge; *hope* and the corresponding gift of fear; *charity* and the corresponding gift of wisdom. Next there follows a treatment of the moral or *cardinal virtues: prudence*, perfected by the gift of counsel; *justice* with its many annexed virtues, among which is the virtue of religion, and the corresponding gift of piety; *courage* and the corresponding gift of courage; *temperance* with chastity as one of its an-nexed virtues and the intervention of the gift of fear.

This moral theology, directed to all people, is brought to completion in a special section devoted to the *charisms*, principally to prophecy, and to the special states of life in the Church, such as the episcopate and religious life.

Structure of the Moral Theology of Saint Thomas
The Second Part of the *Summa theologiae*
The Return of Humans toward God

Prima secundae: general treatment
Happiness and the ultimate end: qq. 1–5
Voluntary Action:
    its nature: qq. 6–10
    analysis: qq. 11–17
    goodness and malice: qq. 18–21
    The Passions: qq. 22–48

The internal principles of human acts
The Virtues
    the habits: qq. 49–54
    the virtues: nature, species, conditions: qq. 55–67
    the gifts of the Holy Spirit: q. 68
    the Beatitudes: q. 69
    the fruits of the Holy Spirit: q. 70
Vices and Sins: qq. 71–89

The external principles of human acts
Law
    in general: qq. 90–92
    the eternal law: q. 93
    the natural law: q. 94
    the Old Law: qq. 98–105
    the New or Evangelical Law: qq. 106–8
Grace: qq. 109–14

Secunda secundae: particular treatment
A study of the virtues in particular, organized around the three theological
virtues and the four cardinal virtues. Each virtue is studied in conjunction with
a corresponding gift of the Holy Spirit, the sins that are opposed to it and the
precepts of the Ten Commandments that concern it (as well as any virtues that
might be annexed to it).
Faith with the gifts of intelligence and knowledge: qq. 1–16
Hope with the gift of fear: qq. 17–22
Charity with the gift of wisdom: qq. 23–46
Prudence with the gift of counsel: qq. 47–56
Justice with the virtue of religion and the gift of piety: qq. 57–122
Courage with the gift of courage: qq. 123–40
Temperance with chastity and the gift of fear: qq. 141–70

Special section
Special graces: prophecy, charisms, etc.: qq. 171–78
States of life: the episcopate and religious life: qq. 179–89

N.B. the *Summa theologiae* contains three parts, of which the second is divided into
two subparts: the *Prima secundae* and the *Secunda secundae* (I-II and II-II). All three
parts are divided into questions and these are subdivided into articles.

In the case of St. Thomas, we are clearly dealing with a morality of happiness, virtues, and gifts. It joins together in a remarkable way the Christian heritage (based on the Gospel and developed by the Fathers of the Church) and human wisdom (Aristotle being considered as the best witness of this wisdom).

The point of contact is found in the desire for happiness: in the aspiration for truth and goodness placed by God at the heart of spiritual nature to lead it to God and prepare it to receive the light of revelation with its promises of grace. This is the theme of the natural desire to see God, a central notion in the thought of the Angelic Doctor that subsequently will be much discussed. Following Christian experience, St. Thomas shows how much the desire for God resides secretly in the consciousness of every person. It rests at the root of the moral life and cannot be fulfilled by any good except God himself in a gratuitous gift. In this way, nature and grace are pre-tuned to each other by a foundational harmony composed of the two notes of truth and goodness that form our spiritual being.

The teaching of St. Thomas, therefore, unites in a remarkable manner the power of reason and the insights of contemplative experience in the knowledge of faith. His work justly continues even in our own time to be a classical model and point of reference for theology and even for philosophy. Since the fourteenth century, however, the edifice in moral theology that Aquinas so carefully constructed has been overturned and replaced by a profoundly different conception, one that still deeply influences us.

Principal Scholastic Theologians

Peter Abelard (1079–1142), French. Initiator of the scholastic method, cause of the extension into the Latin Quarter of the cathedral school of Notre Dame, which will become the University of Paris.

Peter Lombard (c. 1100–1160), the "Master of the Sentences." Author and compiler of the *Sentences of the Fathers*, a synthesis of theology, adopted as a textbook by the universities and commented upon by all candidates for masterships in theology.

Secular Masters:
Philip the Chancellor (c. 1160–1230), French. Chancellor of the University of Paris, author of the *Summa de bono*.

William of Auxerre (d. 1231), French. Author of the *Summa aurea*.

Franciscan School

Alexander of Hales (1180–1245), English. The "Irrefutable Doctor." Author, with a team of Franciscans, of the first summation of theology or *Summa theologiae*. Offers a morality grounded more on the commandments than on the virtues.

St. Bonaventure (1221–1274), Tuscan. The "Seraphic Doctor," or "Devout Doctor." Author of *The Journey of the Mind to God*. Minister General and promoter of the Order of St. Francis.

John Duns Scotus (c. 1264–1308), Scottish. The "Subtle Doctor." Adversary of the Theology of St. Thomas Aquinas. Proclaims the primacy of the will. Buried in Cologne.

William of Ockham (c. 1295–1349), English. The "Venerable (or Glorious) Inceptor." Adversary of John XXII, who calls him to Avignon as a result of his teachings offered at Oxford. He took refuge in Bavaria in 1328. He is the initiator of Nominalism, proclaiming a freedom of indifference and a morality of obligation.

Dominican School

St. Albert the Great (1193–1280), Swabian. The "Universal Doctor." One of those who introduced the works of Aristotle into the university curriculum. He composed works in every domain of human knowledge: in theology, philosophy, and the natural sciences. Buried in Cologne.

St. Thomas Aquinas (1225–1274), Neapolitan. The "Angelic Doctor." The principal representative of scholastic theology. Author of the *Summa theologiae*, *Summa contra gentiles*, of commentaries on the Gospel of John, the Letters of St. Paul, the works of Aristotle, of numerous *Disputed Questions* and of numerous minor works. Canonized at Avignon by John XXII in 1323. Buried in Toulouse.

Thomist School

A school formed above all by commentators on the works of St. Thomas, among whom were:

John Capreolus (d. 1444), French. The "Prince of Thomists." Author of a commentary on Peter Lombard's *Sentences*.

Sylvester of Ferrara (1474–1526). Taught at Bologna. Author of a commentary on the *Summa contra gentiles*.

Thomas de Vio (Cajetan) (1469–1526). Taught in Italy. Principal commentator on the *Summa theologiae* of St. Thomas. Master of the Dominican Order and a Cardinal. One of Luther's Roman interlocutors.

Dominican School of Rhineland Mysticism

Meister Eckhart (1260–1327), **Henry Suso** (c. 1294–1366), **John Tauler** (c. 1300–1361)

IV

The Modern Period
The Manuals of Moral Theology

Moralities of Obligation

The end of the Middle Ages was a period of great upheaval in all domains: religious, demographic, and political. This was particularly the case in theology, which saw the emergence of nominalism initiated by the Francis-can William of Ockham (c. 1295–1349). During this period, moral theology focused more and more on the relationship between law and liberty, viewing it from the perspective of obligation.

St. Thomas, like the Fathers, clearly recognized the existence of moral obligations, but he subordinated them to the virtues. In the new conception the relationship is reversed: Obligation is given priority and invades the entire domain of the moral life. This period marks the birth of what can properly be called the "morality of obligation." Later this morality will be embodied in moralities of duty and moral imperatives, for which Immanuel Kant will provide the model in philosophy.

From the end of the Middle Ages, this conception of morality, along with nominalism, spread throughout the universities. It was part of what became known as the "*Via Moderna*," a movement generally accepted by the various schools of theology in spite of the differences existing between them. In the seventeenth century, the morality of obligation also inspired the manuals of moral theology. In the aftermath of the Council of Trent, these manuals were designed for use in seminaries, especially in preparing priests for the pastoral celebration of the sacrament of Penance. The Jesuits were early promoters of the manuals; the prototype of the genre was a work by the Spanish Jesuit, Juan Azor (1536–1603), entitled *Institutiones morales.* The authors of these manuals clearly intended to follow St. Thomas. Yet, animated by the desire to provide a simplified moral teaching accessible to priests and people, they developed a new way of presenting morality. This new method of presentation is reflected in the general format that all the manualists with some variation follow.

They divide moral theology into two parts: fundamental moral theology, which treats the foundational principles, and special moral theology, which considers in detail the laws determining what is permitted or forbidden and governing the resolution of cases of conscience. Fundamental moral theology contains four treatises: laws, human acts, conscience, and sins. Comparing this structure with the structure of St. Thomas' *Summa theologiae,* one notes immediately the disappearance of the treatise on happiness and the ultimate end, as well as the absence of a treatment of the virtues and the gifts. Moreover, a treatise on conscience has been inserted that will henceforth occupy a central place. Lastly, the treatise on grace has been removed from the domain of morals and placed in dogmatic theology.

If one examines the core that governs the structure of this morality, one can distinguish five essential elements analogous to the parts of an atom. This morality contains two poles, one positive, the other negative: In contrast to a *freedom* that generates human acts and that is viewed as a freedom of indifference, there is *law* that limits freedom by means of obligation. The advent of law is what creates morality properly so called. Interaction between these two poles is established by *conscience*, a neutral particle, that functions as a judge applying law to acts to be done or already accomplished. The role of conscience is essential because it enables one to move from the universality of law to the singularity of acts. These acts are considered in the context of their particular circumstances and viewed as cases of conscience, from which the term casuistry – the study of cases – is derived. Lastly, *sins*, to a certain extent, become the privileged domain of moral theology, both because they constitute the matter of the sacrament of Penance and because they are more directly the concern of law in its restrictive action. At the core of this conception of morality, monopolizing all its energy, is the idea and the sentiment of *obligation*.

As the source of morality, law reigns over the entire domain of morality. It is henceforth understood as an edict of a legislative will and no longer as a work of wisdom. Morality is reduced to the voluntary interaction between two freedoms. Reason now has no other function in the moral life than to reveal the law, which gives particular importance to the text that promulgates the law. The study of law, so full and varied in St. Thomas, focuses in the manuals on the Ten Commandments, viewed as an expression of the natural law. The natural law, written by God in the conscience of each person, according to the teaching of St. Paul in the letter to the *Romans* (1.21; 2.26–27), becomes the solid base upon which moral theology is constructed. The Ten Commandments, understood as a code of ethical obligations, provide the primary criteria of judgment and furnish the principal subdivisions of the subject matter.

Special Moral Theology

After presenting the foundations of the moral life, the manualists quite naturally distribute the vast material of

34

moral theology according to the Ten Commandments of God, completed in conjunction with the five commandments of the Church.* Normally, they would add to this a brief presentation of the obligations that each theological virtue imposes, followed by a much longer analysis of the obligations tied to the administration of the sacraments,

Structure of the Moral Theology of St. Alphonsus Liguori	
Topics	**Pages per Topic**
Book One: the rule of human acts	
I. Conscience	68 pages
II. Laws	223 pages
Book Two: precepts concerning the theological virtues:	73 pages
faith (17 pages)	
hope (2 pages)	
charity (51 pages)	
Book Three: precepts of the Ten Commandments and of the Church	781 pages
Book Four: particular precepts concerning religious life, clerics and the laity	246 pages
Book Five: knowledge and discernment of sins	81 pages
I. human acts in general	15 pages
II. sins	63 pages
Book Six: sacraments	1095 pages
Book Seven: ecclesiastical censures and irregularities	252 pages

Theologia moralis
(Rome: Typographia Vaticana, 1905–1912)

Note that the four treatises on fundamental moral theology are intertwined with special moral theology in Books One and Five. They are normally treated separately in the manuals. Note also that the index of this classic work of moral theology does not mention happiness.

---

* These are: (1) to keep Sunday and Holy days of obligation holy by attending Mass, (2) to receive the Eucharist at least once a year at Easter, (3) to confess one's sins in the sacrament of Penance at least one a year, (4) to abstain from meat on Fridays and other days of abstinence, and (5) to fast during Lent and other fast days of the year.

especially Penance and the Eucharist. There would then follow two concluding chapters, one on ecclesiastical censures and penalties and another on the obli$_{b}$ ᵗions proper to those in religious life.

Lastly, many moralists would illustrate their teaching by adding a collection of cases of conscience. These collections would contain difficult cases that enabled the manualists to apply their insights. These authors would either place the cases at the end of each section of their work, referencing them to the material just covered, or they would dedicate a special separate volume to these cases.

The Question of Probabilism

The problem that absorbed the attention of moralists during the century of Descartes (1596–1650) was the issue of doubt in applying laws to particular actions. How should one proceed when one is in doubt about the law itself or about the circumstances surrounding the action? This issue divided moralists into different schools according to the "systems of morality" they advocated as the solution. The debate was triggered by the following question: In a case of doubt, may one follow a probable (*probabilis*) opinion in favor of freedom, even if a contrary opinion favoring the law has more arguments in favor of it and is thus more probable (*probabilior*)? Probability was measured by internal and above all by external arguments. Specifically, it was determined by following the number and authority of the moralists who held such an opinion. Moralists who affirmed that one could follow an opinion that was simply probable were called "probabilists." Those who maintained that one must always follow the more probable opinion were called "probabiliorists."

This discussion, which ultimately called into question all judgments in moral theology, gave birth to several excesses. On one side there was *laxism*, which was too

36

favorable toward freedom; on the other there was *rigorism* or *tutiorism,* according to which one should always follow the opinion that favors the law. The controversy lasted three centuries and reached a point of equilibrium in the system of St. Alphonsus Liguori (1696–1787), who held that there was no such thing as a true quandary and that one could not follow an opinion favorable to freedom unless there were at least as many arguments in its favor as there were in favor of the contrary opinion, a view that came to be called "equiprobabilism." Because of this sagacious insight, Alphonsus would be proclaimed the patron of moral theologians.

Assessment

The manuals of moral theology formed a tradition that one was justified in calling "Catholic" morality. Since the Council of Trent, the manuals have truly played an important role in the life of the Church. Their doctrine, which was taught in the seminaries, was written into the catechisms and poured into the Church's preaching and pastoral practice of the sacraments. It was also embedded in the examinations of conscience that were offered to the faithful to follow.

An appraisal of the manuals must be nuanced. Without question they essentially fulfilled the function demanded of them: to teach priests and faithful the fundamental moral principles and the necessary commandments of morality (both natural and Christian), and to explain how to apply them. In constructing their works, the manualists took as their foundation the Ten Commandments and the natural law. By doing so, they were being faithful both to the Church and to the humanism of the modern era. No one who wishes to build a solid construction in moral theology can abandon such a foundation. It is also necessary to add that in the heart of the

---

The Tradition of Manuals of Moral Theology

Origins

Bartolomé de Medina, Spanish Dominican (1528–1581). *Breve instrucción de comme se ha administrar el sacramento de la penitencia.* "Father of probabilism": the view that one can follow a probable opinion, even if the opinion favoring the law is more probable.

Juan Azor, Spanish Jesuit (1536–1603), professor at Rome. Composed the *Institutiones morales,* following the new regulations governing studies in the Society of Jesus. This work is the first example of the format that will be adopted by the manuals of moral theology. It organizes moral theology according to the commandments of God and of the Church.

Seventeenth Century

Hermann Busenbaum, German Jesuit (1600–1668). He wrote the *Medulla theologiae moralis,* which will be used by St. Alphonsus.

Juan Caramuel y Lobkowitz, Spanish Cistercian (1606–1668). "The Prince of the Laxists," according to St. Alphonsus.

Antonino Diana, Italian Theatine (1585–1663). In his *Resolutiones morales,* he resolves some 30,000 cases.

Antonio Escobar y Mendoza, Spanish Jesuit (1589–1669). Vigorously attacked by Pascal in *Les Provinciales.*

Paul Laymann, German Jesuit (1575–1635). He was a moralist and a canonist and author of the influential *Theologia moralis.*

Tomás Sanchez, Spanish Jesuit (1550–1610). He wrote a work based on the Ten Commandments. Taken to task by Pascal.

Tommaso Tamburini, Italian Jesuit (1591–1675). *Expeditae decalogi explicationes.* Had a broad perspective: held that one could follow a probably probable opinion.

Blaise Pascal (1623–1662). In *Les Provinciales* he attacks the excesses of the probabilists.

Alexandre Noël [Natalis], French Dominican (1639–1724). A vigorous adversary of probabilism.

Eighteenth Century

St. Alphonsus Liguori, Italian, founder of the Redemptorists (1696–1787). Doctor of the Church, patron of moral theologians. *Theologia moralis* in 4 volumes. Advocates the system of equiprobabilism.

Giovanni Vincenzo Patuzzi, Italian Dominican (1700–1769). Adversary of probabilism; critic of St. Alphonsus.

Charles-René Billuart, Belgian Dominican (1685–1757). Commentator of St. Thomas who guided many authors of manuals and of works "according to the mind of St. Thomas." He was a moderate probabiliorist.

Nineteenth Century

Josef Aertnijs, Dutch Redemptorist (1828–1915). *Theologia moralis juxta doctrinam S. Alphonsi* and *Theologia pastoralis.*

Édouard Génicot, Belgian Jesuit (1858–1900). *Theologiae moralis institutiones* with a volume of "cases of conscience." Revised later by Josef Salsmans.

Jean-Pierre Gury, French Jesuit (1801–1866). *Compendium theologiae moralis* with "cases of conscience." This manual was probably the most widely used manual of the nineteenth century. Widely read in America in the revised version composed by Aloysius Sabetti, s.J. (1839–1898).

August Lehmkuhl, German Jesuit (1837–1917). *Theologia moralis* with "cases of conscience." Defender of probabilism.

Clément Marc, French Redemptorist (1831–1887). *Institutiones morales alphonsianae.*

Jerome Noldin, Austrian Jesuit (1818–1922). *Summa theologiae moralis.* 3 volumes.

Twentieth Century

Heribert Jone, German Capuchin (1885–1967). *Moral Theologie.* Written in German and translated into English as *Moral Theology* (Westminster, Md.: Newman Press, 1963). Much employed and very juridical.

Benoît-Henri Merkelbach, Belgian Dominican (1871–1942). *Summa theologiae moralis,* 3 volumes. A work centered on the virtues from the perspective of St. Thomas.

Dominic Prümmer, German Dominican (1866–1931). *Manuale theologiae moralis,* 3 volumes. Adopts the order of the virtues. His pocket sized *Vademecum theologiae moralis* was translated into English as *Handbook of Moral Theology* (New York: P. J. Kennedy, 1957).

Arthur Vermeersch, Belgian Jesuit (1898–1936). *Theologiae moralis principia, responsa, consilia.* Reprinted by J. Creusen.

N.B. – Since they were written for the education of clerics, the moral manuals were generally written in Latin.

Church, the work of these moralists was normally enriched by its contact with the works of spiritual authors and of the saints. Moralists in this way secured for the Christian people a first-rate moral education that was precise, clear, comprehensible to all, and that guaranteed the essentials. We must, therefore, respect this labor of four centuries and only critique it with care and discernment.

The Second Vatican Council, however, continues to invite us to engage in renewal and offers us the means for doing so. We live at a time when the foundations of morality have been shaken in our societies, and the need to recover moral principles is everywhere apparent. At such a time, we should not hesitate to point out the limitations of the teachings of the manuals so that we may recover a Christian morality that is complete in all its dimensions and enjoys its full force and attraction.

The primary reproach that one can make against the moralities of obligation (such as the moralities of duties, imperatives, norms, etc.) is that they have restricted considerably the domain of moral theology. Because of its focus on obligations, moral theology has detached itself from everything that goes beyond legal imperatives: from the search for perfection, which is henceforth reserved to an elite; from the interior mystical movement of the heart so closely linked to love; and from spirituality in general. The moral theology of the manuals lost sight of essential questions: the treatise on happiness and the destiny of the human person; the treatises on the Evangelical Law, on grace, and on the gifts of the Holy Spirit. All these treatises disappeared from the manuals. Obedience to law encroached upon charity and the virtues; the theme of friendship was lost; the social and ecclesial dimensions of the Christian life were neglected. Moral theology's relationship with the Scriptures was reduced to rare citations, having set aside the richest and most powerful passages of the Gospel. Its relationship to faith suffered because of an exaggerated separation between dogma and morals. The pastoral practice of the sacraments and of the liturgy was scarcely considered by moral theology except from a juridical perspective. The challenge of renewal in Catholic moral theology, therefore, is to return to the foundations of morality and to restore to moral theology its full breadth, both on the level of human experience and in its use of Christian revelation.

V

The Question of Christian Ethics after the Council

The post-councilor period caused much turmoil and called into question traditional doctrines on a number of points, especially in the area of moral theology. This questioning has brought to the fore a fundamental issue: What is the contribution of faith and Christianity to moral teaching, to what is often called "ethics"? Stated another way, does a specifically Christian ethics exist?

In the past this question would have appeared insolent, if not scandalous, because Catholic moral teaching seemed, even in the eyes of non-believers, to be the most solid and educationally useful part of the Church's teaching. Moreover, people generally did not give much credence to secular moralities based purely on reason alone. The backing of the God of revelation and the authority of the Church were viewed as necessary elements of any effort to place the rules of the moral life on a firm foundation.

The Second Vatican Council introduced important changes in this regard. First, it gave Catholics new and unreserved access to the Scriptures, the liturgy, and the spiritual and patristic traditions of the Church. The Council thus fostered a renewal in the Christian dimension of its moral teaching by encouraging moral theologians to draw on these rich sources. It is from this perspective that we shall attempt to show how faith offers a specific response to the great moral questions.

At the same time, however, the Council renewed the Church's attitude toward the modern world, fostering what became known as "openness to the world." It did so by acknowledging the goodness of every level of human values – the level of the sciences, philosophy, politics, and society, etc. – in an effort to establish a true dialogue with the peoples of contemporary culture. This has caused a change of perspective among moralists, who increasingly are giving more attention to the human dimension of their discipline, particularly to human relations and the sciences that study them, such as psychology and sociology. Without doubt this has enriched the Church's ethical reflection and broadened its perspective. Yet it is necessary to engage in such reflection judiciously and not abandon the solid insights offered by Christian doctrine. Moreover, in order to avoid misunderstanding and confusion, one has to delineate with care the domains and the methods proper to each science.

Developments in science and technology have also raised new questions. These developments have altered the human environment, changed lifestyles, modified customary practices, and have required particularly delicate modifications in the civil legislation of our societies, societies that have become thoroughly pluralistic. The formulation of a Christian response to concrete problems has become urgent. The issues of contraception, divorce, abortion, euthanasia, homosexuality, the pollution of the environment, and, most recently, AIDS, all call for an articulate and balanced Christian response.

Viewed in its entirety, therefore, the question of Christian ethics has two facets. There is first a directly Christian dimension stemming from the more intense relationship now existing between ethics and the Scriptures, between ethics and the Gospel. Next, there is a human dimension stemming from the new relationship

The Council and the Teaching of Moral Theology

Special care should be given to the perfecting of moral theology. Its scientific presentation should draw more fully on the teaching of Holy Scripture and should throw light upon the exalted vocation of the faithful in Christ and their obligation to bring forth fruit in charity for the life of the world.

Vatican II
Optatam Totius
Decree on the Training of Priests, n. 16

Moral theology has at times in the past exhibited a certain narrowness of focus and contained lacunae in its perspective. This was in great part due to a certain legalism and individualism, as well as to a separation from the sources of Revelation. To overcome all of this it becomes necessary to clarify the epistemological status of moral theology. It is necessary, therefore, to determine how to construct moral theology in close contact with Holy Scripture, Tradition – received through faith and interpreted by the Magisterium – and in reference to the natural law known by reason.

On this basis, a renewal of moral theology should be possible, a renewal that restores its spiritual, pastoral, and "political" application. . . . With this aim in view, it is necessary, above all, to have a lively awareness of the link between moral and dogmatic theology. . . . With regard to this, we would do well to return to the perspective of St. Thomas Aquinas, who, like other great masters, never separated moral from dogmatic theology. On the contrary, he placed it within the unitary plan of systematic theology, viewing it as the study of the process by which the human person, created in the likeness of God and redeemed by the grace of Christ, tends toward his full realization, according to the demands of his divine calling, in the context of the economy of salvation historically realized in the Church.

Congregation for Catholic Education
Document on the Theological Formation of Future Priests
(22 February 1976) 3.2.4

existing between Christian ethics, philosophy, and the sciences. It is a relationship existing on the level of reason and is precisely the level at which the tradition placed the natural law.

The question of Christian ethics was introduced into the Church by the new currents of thought – in biblical studies, patristics, liturgy, and spirituality – that prepared for the Second Vatican Council and were subsequently confirmed by the Council. Yet the problem was primarily posed on the level of the rational dimension of ethics, something which scholasticism after the Council of Trent had already strongly emphasized.

One began to ask the following question: Since Christian ethics as presented in the manuals of theology is primarily a series of commandments or norms that in principle are accessible to human reason, what specific contribution can divine revelation make to it? Stated in another way, does the New Testament contain moral norms that are not found anywhere else, neither in the Old Testament, nor in other religions, nor in the teachings of the philosophers? By phrasing the question in this way, ethicists began to search for a Christian remainder or residue; yet, since they employed a method that concentrated only on a narrow aspect of the Gospel, they ran the risk of finding very little. It would have been better to compare Christian doctrine in its totality with other totalities, such as Jewish ethics, Greek ethics, or philosophical ethics. One would thus have been in a position to compare the contours of one with the contours of another. Nevertheless, though rudimentary, the process they employed had the advantage of being simple and gave the appearance of being easy to use.

Lastly, we should note an event that has played a striking role in subsequent debates among moralists: the publication by Paul VI on 25 July 1968 of the encyclical

Humanae vitae and the position it takes against the use of artificial forms of contraception. This decision about a particular problem has provoked profound reactions. These reactions became progressively more far-reaching in their implications, even to the point of calling into question the very principles underlying traditional Catholic moral theology.

Does a Christian Ethics Exist?
A Response

We shall begin by presenting one answer to this question that has received much attention among moral theologians. It is the response that Josef Fuchs offers in his book *Existe-t-il une morale chrétienne?* (Gembloux: J. Duculot, 1973), a work that touches on all aspects of the question. According to Fuchs, one should distinguish two levels or parts in Catholic morality. First of all, Catholic morality teaches general attitudes that engage the whole person, such as faith, love, the imitation of Christ, and the acceptance of salvation. Employing technical language evocative of Aristotle and Kant, Fuchs calls this level the "transcendental level." Scripture expresses these attitudes with great frequency and clarity. Clearly, on this level the moral teaching of the Church is specifically Christian.

But Catholic moral theology also considers actions that concern limited areas, such as justice, social life, temperance, chastity, or marriage. Concrete actions and cases of conscience can fall into different categories, the judgment of which is primarily the concern of reason because biblical directives in these areas are more rare and less clear. This is what is called the "categorical level." Fuchs contends that if one considers Christian ethics from this perspective, viewing it as a teaching that proposes universal human values, then it is essentially a human ethics and not specifically Christian, although the ambience that surrounds it will be Christian.

The response to our question, therefore, is nuanced. Is there a Christian ethics? If one considers Christian ethics *from the perspective of general transcendental attitudes, the answer is yes.* If, on the other hand, one considers it *from the perspective of categorical behavior, the answer is no*; Christian ethics, on the level of its material content, is merely a human ethics.

This skillful solution has advantages and disadvantages. In the tradition of Renaissance humanism, which has deeply influenced Catholic teaching, this response emphasizes the human dimension and universal significance of ethics, traits that are particularly valued in our world today, where peoples and civilizations are coming into contact as never before. This response brings to the fore in Catholic ethics the common denominator of reason and the norms for addressing cases of conscience as well as the new problems that confront us on both the individual and legislative levels.

The distinction that this response proposes, however, has the damaging effect of fostering a separation between the Christian and the human dimensions of morality that reside at the heart of Catholic ethics and, in a certain sense, cuts them in two. As a result, it becomes difficult to see what contribution Christianity makes to ethics on the categorical level, to the domain of norms and the concrete problems upon which ethical debates actually focus. It seems that these questions can and even should essentially be treated solely on the level of human values and rational arguments. From this perspective Christianity merely provides a special inspiration, a favorable climate or a context that places ethical problems in a religious framework; yet, as such, Christianity will always remain exterior to moral judgments, being, as it were, on the margins of ethics.

The Demand for the Autonomy of Ethics

The problem of the relationship between the Christian and human dimensions of Catholic ethics becomes more pronounced following the Church's "openness to the world" and to modern thought, as this openness has been practiced in the aftermath of the Council. Two issues in this regard have particularly important implications for ethics.

Influenced by the radical distinction established by Kant between heteronomous ethics, which places the source of law in a will external to the human person, and autonomous ethics, which makes the imperative of law spring from the human person's own reason, there has arisen among Catholic ethicists, especially in German-speaking countries, a growing demand for the autonomy of ethics. In the aftermath of the encyclical *Humanae vitae*, this current has turned its attention to considering the legitimacy of the Magisterium's interventions and its authority in the domain of ethics.

Conscious of its mission to transmit and safeguard the Gospel message in the area of faith and morals, the Magisterium of the Church claims for itself the power to speak authoritatively, not only about the content of Christian revelation, but also about moral questions rooted in the natural law and thus belonging to the realm of reason. This claim is founded on the close and necessary connection between the message of the Gospel and the principles of the natural law. It is also founded on the recognition that human reason is often dimmed either from weakness or from the effects of sin and thus needs reinforcement. In fact, the natural law as expressed in the Ten Commandments has always been the principal foundation of the Church's moral teaching. In other words, the Church does not believe that it can neglect anything that is human, anything that promotes the dignity of the human person. Pope Paul VI even asserted that the Church should be "an expert in humanity."

The debate over the Magisterium's competence in the area of the natural law has important implications. As a debate that addresses specific cases as well as universal principles, it draws to the fore the distinction between transcendental and categorical ethics questioned above. Is it possible in the name of the autonomy of ethics to deny the Church and its Magisterium the right to intervene with special authority in discussions concerning contemporary ethical problems? The inadmissibility of such a claim becomes evident once we recognize that, although one can theoretically and in the abstract separate the orders of faith and reason, of grace and nature, human actions as concretely lived and experienced unite these two realms. Existentially, the human act brings the two realms together to form an integral whole. As Maurice Blondel has pointed out, all voluntary action, whether one recognizes it or not, implicitly poses the question of God, and hence of faith and the supernatural. Because of this, in accord with its vocation, the Church has an important role to play in the activities that engage Christians as humans and as believers.

We see, therefore, that the assertion that there is no such thing as a specifically Christian ethics has precise implications. If the demand for the autonomy of ethics leads us to restrict to reason alone the task of solving ethical problems, then in the final analysis the Church and faith itself will no longer have much of a role in the moral life; they will merely represent one opinion among others, and will, moreover, always be viewed with suspicion as being an authoritarian imposition. The "Christian climate" of the culture will do little to change this.

Abandonment of the Natural Law in Light of Modern Philosophy and the Sciences

This vast debate has had a further consequence. Since moral theologians after the Council were newly attentive to the rational character of their discipline, one would have expected them to preserve and develop the theory of the natural law as the cornerstone of their thought. It would have been logical for them to view the natural law as the firm foundation upon which to build the structure of the moral life. In fact, however, a facile openness to modern thought coupled with an allergic reaction against casuistry led them to abandon this resource. The project of engaging modern thought required daring and deep discernment. Sadly, these traits were often lacking. Many moralists were content to conform the Church's moral teaching to "modernity," often retaining only scattered elements of this teaching, which they arranged as they saw fit or according to the reigning opinion. As a result, Catholic moral theology was in danger of disintegrating. Indeed, how can one retain the doctrine of the natural law when one embraces currents of thought that set aside universal, stable human nature and give primacy to existential decision, historical evolution or to social struggle and cultural pluralism? When nature is placed in opposition to progress in thought and growth in freedom, nature becomes something to subdue and is no longer viewed as an interior rule to follow.

What remain are the sciences and technology, which exert a sort of fascination upon us by their discoveries and their successes. Moralists have been particularly attracted to the human sciences, to psychology, psychoanalysis, sociology, and most recently to biology and the problems arising in medicine and genetics. Such knowledge is truly useful, even necessary, in order to make adequate judgments concerning the human person and the context of his actions. Here again, however, discernment is indispensable. One cannot simply import into moral theology without modification the methods and categories of the human sciences. The research of sociologists, for example, can enlighten us concerning the mores of a people in a certain context, but it cannot change the nature of morality, as if moral teaching were like civil laws that we can change whenever the majority desires to do so. In fact, it often happens that the resistance of a small group, or even of one person, prevails because of the authenticity of their testimony in favor of a specific moral value. Similarly, without doubt, analysis of the stages of psychological development from infancy to adulthood, sheds light on the formation of the human personality; but on its own this analysis cannot account for moral experience, which is already present in the young (sometimes with greater clarity than in adults); nor can this analysis establish the rules of morality.

The fundamental difference between moral theology and the human sciences resides in the different methodological attitudes they require. The sciences employ a method of observation that treats human behavior as a "fact" before which the researcher, in the name of objectivity, must maintain a certain distance and neutrality. These sciences attain exterior knowledge, knowledge of the observable or of what the philosophers call the "phenomena." They do not claim to determine, nor can they determine, what "should be done," what should be according to the nature of things. They are not normative, nor will they ever be able to construct an ethics. Moral experience, for its part, differs from scientific experience because moral experience is interior. One only grasps the nature and core meaning of moral experience by reflecting upon one's own personal engagement in human actions. If scientific observation requires cold objectivity, moral perception requires the warm flame of action. The principal method in morals, therefore, is to reflect on the act itself and on its free source within us, which is made known to us interiorly. This is the meaning of the Socratic dictum, "know yourself." It is here, at the heart of one's active conscience, that the moral law becomes most evident to us, for it is here that the moral law reigns. Thus, moral knowledge is essentially normative. More than a science, it is a wisdom.

We must also carefully distinguish the moral law from scientific laws drawn from observation. They belong to two different orders. Hence, we should not expect the sciences to demonstrate the truth of a natural law in the moral order. By the same token, however, it would be a grave mistake to abandon the doctrine of the natural law merely because it isn't "scientific." Indeed, scientists themselves increasingly are recognizing that on their own science and technology are not sufficient when it is the human person that is at stake. The problems that confront us today are drawing ethics and the sciences into ever deeper contact. They challenge us to delineate more clearly the relationship that should exist between science and ethics so that a fruitful cooperation can be fostered between them.

Question of Intrinsically Evil Acts and Universal Laws

We shall complete our portrait by saying a few words about a debate that continues to polarize moral theologians today: the question of intrinsically evil acts and the system of moral analysis called "proportionalism" or "consequentialism."

The question of intrinsically evil acts arose in the wake of the discussions concerning Christian ethics that we outlined above, and like them, is linked historically to the controversies surrounding the encyclical *Humanae vitae*. The term "intrinsically evil acts" refers to acts that are in themselves morally evil, independently of any circumstance or situation, and therefore they are acts which one can never do. (See S. Pinckaers, *Ce qu'on ne peut jamais faire* [Fribourg, Switzerland: Éditions Universitaires Fribourg, 1986]). The question is whether such acts exist.

Examples of intrinsically evil acts are: lying, according to St. Augustine and Kant; artificial contraception, according to the encyclical *Humanae vitae*; abortion and torture, and so forth. Any attempt, however, to generate a list of such acts immediately broadens the discussion because judgments concerning particular acts depend on concrete norms and general principles, such as the Ten Commandments. We can, therefore, pose the question as follows. Are there moral laws that are universally true and valid at all times, places, and situations, such that it would always be a moral fault to violate them? This question leads us back to the natural law and how it applies in concrete cases.

Pope Pius XII had already addressed this problem in his critique of "situation ethics," an ethics which argued that it belonged to each person's conscience to judge according to a hierarchy of personal values whether or not a universal law applied in a concrete situation ("Address to the World Federation of Young Women," 18 April 1952). Yet, after the Second Vatican Council, the debate took a new form.

Briefly, those who are often called "Revisionists" locate moral judgment in the comparing or balancing of the good and evil effects that an action causes in a given situation in relation to the end pursued. Everything depends upon the proportion established between the consequences of an act, and hence the name "proportionalism" or "consequentialism" is given to this system of moral analysis.

It is indeed true that concrete actions often cause contrary effects. Building a factory generates wealth and jobs, but it also damages the environment. A medicine necessary for the health of the patient can also have unwanted side effects. An action done with the best of intentions can sometimes have damaging results. It seems, therefore, that in general one can apply to human action a method of calculating the proportion between good and evil effects. Moreover, in order to form an adequate judgment, it will be necessary to take into account, as much as possible, all the intervening circumstances and the resulting consequences in varying degrees of distance from the action itself.

The Revisionists, however, clarify that this judgment is preliminary and resides on what they call the "pre-moral" level. The act will acquire moral value when the will accepts the act in its relation to the moral law. Hence, they distinguish the level of "rightness" from the level of "goodness."

With regard to the moral law, the source of moral obligation, these authors give special attention to how it has been formulated and applied in various different ways by different cultures and at different times over the course of history. The Revisionists take particular care to identify closely the concrete norms that govern an action, even in its particularity.

One last thing that we should note: "Proportionalism" is listed among the "teleological" systems of moral analysis that are opposed to "deontological" forms of analysis. Proportionalism locates the moral value of an act in its relationship to the end intended, viewing the act as a means of attaining an end. (In Greek, *telos* means end; hence the name "teleology.") The moral value of the act is thus relative to the end. On the other hand, deontological forms of analysis, following the Kantian model, hold that an act can be absolutely good or evil, independently of the circumstances, including the end sought.

By giving priority in moral judgment to the relationship between the human act, viewed as a means to an end, and the effects it causes, proportionalism is well suited to the technical mentality of our age. The pre-moral level that proportionalism describes as the essential locus of judgment greatly resembles the domain proper to the technical arts. This explains the popularity that this conception of morality has enjoyed; it also, however, explains why one can level the reproach against it that it is merely a form of utilitarianism.

If one considers the internal logic of proportionalism, it is difficult to see how one can reconcile this system of moral analysis with the recent pronouncements of the Magisterium defending the universality of moral norms and the existence of intrinsically evil acts. Indeed, how can one demonstrate that certain actions are evil in themselves and that certain norms are universally applicable without exception, if one makes moral judgment in each case depend on a battery of objective and subjective circumstances and consequences, many of which are clearly variable? We can always imagine unforeseen circumstances that, by modifying the situation, would be an obstacle to formulating a universal law. At the end of the day, when we are confronted with a difficult moral problem, we can easily believe that we are in a morally unique situation merely from the fact that we are personally implicated in that situation. There is danger here of moral relativism. There is the danger of falling into precisely that form of moral relativism against which the Magisterium of the Church has seen fit to warn the faithful.

Variations of Conscience
Let us note a considerable change in mentality that has affected the role and meaning of conscience. The manuals accord a central place to conscience: It is the intermediary

between law and liberty; it applies the law to specific acts and judges these acts in the name of the law. From this perspective, the primary task of the moralist is to resolve cases of conscience. Conscience thus became the preeminent locus of the moral life. Yet the center of gravity remained in the law, with conscience and moral theologians acting merely as interpreters of the law.

Conscience can, however, exercise a richer and more varied function than merely imposing legal obligations. In the Christian tradition, as explained by Cardinal Newman (1801–1890), for example, conscience signifies the voice of God that resounds in the intimacy of the human heart, one on one. Conscience supremely judges and commands, but it also calls to conversion and traces the often surprising ways that lead to a vocation. Conscience is profoundly personal and yet can form deep bonds of ecclesial communion.

Conscience viewed in this way was what Newman called "the aboriginal vicar of Christ." Nevertheless, already in the nineteenth century Newman pointed out that an important change in meaning was occurring: he noted that for many, an appeal to conscience no longer evoked a reference to an interior Judge, but solely signified "an Englishman's prerogative, to be his own master in all things," without concern for God or for any religious authority whatsoever (*A Letter Addressed to His Grace the Duke of Norfolk on Occasion of Mr. Gladstone's Recent Expostulation* [New York: Catholic Publication Society, 1875], 73 and 75).

In fact, however, conscience looks in two directions. While it looks to God and to the law, it also represents the subject, the personal self of which it is a part. In reaction against excessive legalism, there developed among Catholics in the aftermath of the Council a certain allergic aversion to law, which has shifted the center of gravity in moral theology away from law and toward personal freedom, the individual subject and conscience. Hence, personal conscience tends to become the ultimate judge in the moral life, without one being sufficiently attentive to the ambiguity that arises when one so closely associates conscience with one's personal opinion, which is often self-justifying.

The shift to this view of conscience is made easier for us who live in democratic societies that regularly reach decisions by calculating the majority view. From within this social context, moral theologians are themselves also tempted to resolve problems of conscience by following the strongest current of public opinion. They base their judgments on apparently scientific studies that measure public opinion and reveal majority views, which are in general vested with an authority that is said to be moral.

In this way, diverse opinions (as occurred during the conflicts over probabilism) and subsequent debates between majorities and authorities replace serious study of the principles underlying moral problems that demand competence and experience. In such an atmosphere we are very far from the view of conscience described by Newman: a conscience that makes judgments in the presence of God by listening to his sovereign voice, or perhaps more accurately a conscience that lets itself be judged by God and guided by his law through a fruitful, open, and intelligent obedience. One sign that helps us distinguish true from false conscience is certainly that true conscience always presents a challenge, like the steep and narrow way of the Gospel that stands in stark contrast to the broad and easy way that leads to eternal sorrow. At the same time, true conscience gives to those who follow it a peace and joy that no external thing can trouble, while false conscience without fail provokes doubt and division, compromise and confusion.

Documents of the Magisterium

We shall conclude the first part of our study by noting the principal recent documents of the Magisterium that treat ethical issues.

The encyclical *Humanae vitae* (25 July 1968) condemned artificial means of birth control. The apostolic exhortation of John Paul II, *Familiaris consortio* (22 November 1981), expounds the Christian doctrine of marriage in its entirety: it considers the present situation and the plan of God; the community of persons entrusted with the transmission of life and the education of offspring; participation in the life of society and the mission of the Church at the service of humanity; and the apostolate to the family, especially in the difficult case of divorce and remarriage.

The *Declaration on Euthanasia* by the Congregation for the Doctrine of the Faith (5 May 1980) clarifies and renders more precise the traditional terminology and teaching concerning end-of-life issues in response to new questions posed by advances in medical technology.

The encyclical *Dominum et vivificantem* (18 May 1986), considers the role of the Holy Spirit in the life of the Church and of the world. The Holy Spirit purifies conscience, gives us the grace to overcome the conflict between the spirit and the flesh described by St. Paul, and strengthens in us the "inner man."

The letter issued by the Congregation for the Doctrine of the Faith, *The Pastoral Care of Homosexual Persons* (1 October 1986), deplores the mistreatment that homosexual persons so often suffer, and urges that special pastoral attention be afforded to them. At the same time, it reaffirms the constant teaching of the Church concerning the sinful character of homosexual acts.

The instruction, *Donum vitae* from the Congregation for the Doctrine of the Faith (22 February 1987), considers bioethical questions. It reaffirms the respect due to nascent life and the dignity of procreation. Responding to contemporary questions raised by advances in biotechnology, the letter rejects *in vitro* fertilization as morally illicit, even when it is "homologous," i.e., between husband and wife.

The *Instruction on the Ecclesial Vocation of the Theologian* (24 May 1990) by the Congregation for the Doctrine of the Faith addresses the relationship between moral theologians and the Magisterium, the collaboration that should exist between them, and the cases of dissent that may arise. It charts the levels of authority that different documents of the Magisterium enjoy and the levels of assent that they require.

The Catechism of the Catholic Church, published in October of 1992, presents Christian doctrine in its entirety, through a presentation enriched by constant references to the Scriptures, the Fathers of the Church, theologians from the Middle Ages, especially St. Thomas Aquinas, modern theologians and spiritual authors, as well as to recent documents of the Magisterium. The third part of the *Catechism* is dedicated to the moral life, presenting it from the Gospel perspective as a "life in Christ." The first section considers the vocation of the human person to life in the Spirit, animated by divine charity and human solidarity. It presents fundamental moral theology in a manner much more complete than the one offered by the traditional manuals of moral theology, which limited it to four treatises (law, conscience, human acts, and sins) and focused it on legal obligations.

Instead, beginning with the creation of the human person in the image of God as the ground of human dignity, the *Catechism* situates the moral life in the context of the human person's natural desire for happiness, for which the divine promises and the Evangelical Beatitudes are a response. After presenting the studies on human freedom, on the moral status of human acts, including the passions or emotions, and the treatise on conscience, the *Catechism* restores the study of the virtues to a place of primary importance. It considers both the theological virtues and the natural human virtues, without neglecting the gifts of the Holy Spirit. It also insists upon the social and communal dimensions of the Christian life. The *Catechism* then considers the moral law, firmly establishing the moral law's foundations. It presents the moral law as founded on the natural law and the Ten Commandments, which it describes as ordered to the New Law, expressed in the Sermon on the Mount and defined as the grace of the Holy Spirit. This leads the *Catechism* to reintroduce into moral theology the treatise on grace, presenting grace as "the *free and undeserved help* that God gives us to respond to his call to become children of God . . ." (§1996). It concludes the first section with a study of the Church as the Mother and Teacher of the moral life. We should note also that the *Catechism* reestablishes the close connection between moral and spiritual theology.

In the second section, the *Catechism* divides special moral theology in the classical way, following the precepts of the Ten Commandments. Yet, more effectively than was done in the past, it presents the precepts in relation to the virtues, describing them as a preparation for the exercise of the virtues, especially the love of God and of neighbor.

The *Catechism*, therefore, in a positive way profoundly renews the presentation of Christian morality. It makes the great heritage of Christian doctrine, with all its richness in moral, spiritual, as well as dogmatic theology, accessible to all those who take the time to read it.

The encyclical *Veritatis splendor* (6 August 1993) responds to the crisis in Christian moral theology that arose in the aftermath of the Second Vatican Council, to which we have already referred. Taking as its Gospel foundation the question of the rich young man to Jesus: "Teacher, what good must I do to attain eternal life?" (*Mt* 19.16), the encyclical opposes the demand for the complete autonomy of moral judgment advanced in the name of freedom and human reason. It criticizes the too clearcut distinction proposed between the salvific level of one's primary options in life (the transcendental level), viewed as the level on which properly Christian moral teaching belongs, and the more concrete level of the different categories of action (the categorical level), viewed as the level where moral judgments essentially depend on reason, and where moral judgment is regarded as the comparative calculation of consequences ("consequentialism" or "proportionalism").

The encyclical recognizes that what is at stake in this debate is the permanence of universal moral laws, regarded as applicable at all times and among all peoples. Hence, the encyclical affirms that certain acts are "intrinsically evil," because of their essential objects, such as murder, abortion, adultery, and so forth, regardless of their consequences and secondary circumstances. The Magisterium seeks at all cost to preserve this solid foundation for moral judgment and Christian teaching. Indeed, it understands itself as having the responsibility to do so in the name of the Gospel and of the moral law inscribed by God in the heart of every person.

The encyclical *Evangelium vitae* (25 March 1995) pursues a twofold goal. First, it vigorously defends human life by solemnly condemning abortion, euthanasia, and suicide, which directly violate the precept, "you shall not kill." It denounces in our societies the danger of a "culture of death," against which we must fight on the personal, social, political, and legislative levels, even to the point of conscientious objection, if this becomes necessary. The second goal of the encyclical is to promote a "culture of life," especially on the level of the family, which it calls the "sanctuary of life" that forms the basic unit of society and of the great family that is the Church.

The Truth and Meaning of Human Sexuality, a document of the Pontifical Council on the Family (8 December 1995), offers guidance for sexual education within the family. We should add several discourses of John Paul II. There are, among others, "Biological Experimentation" (23 October 1982); "Prenatal diagnosis and surgery" (4 December 1982); "Dangers of genetic manipulation" (29 October 1983); "Opposing Euthanasia" (6 September 1984); "The Mystery of Life and Death" (21 October 1985). We should note also his *Letter to Families* of 2 February 1994.

All these documents are guided by the same concern: respect for the human person and his or her life from the moment of its conception until death. These documents express a common desire to promote the dignity of all people and to safeguard their fundamental rights in conformity with the natural law.

Part II

A More Difficult Reflection
than One Might Think

VI

Freedom and Happiness

The task that the Council entrusted to moral theologians is not easy, but, as everyone knows, it is urgent. It requires a reexamination of the foundations of moral theology and reflective research on the human person as the agent of his acts. Scripture teaches us that the human person has been created in the image of God. Placing this text from *Genesis* prominently at the head of his moral theology, St. Thomas applies it to the human person's free choice (*liberum arbitrium*). This freedom together with law form the two poles of the moral life; on this point all moralists agree.

Moralities of Happiness and Moralities of Obligation

Problems surface and dissensions arise when we attempt to introduce a third factor into moral theology: the desire for happiness. Suddenly we are confronted with a broader and deeper issue than we expected.

When we study the history of moral analysis, both in theology and in philosophy, we discover that we can divide this history into two great periods. In the first period, which stretches from Antiquity into the Middle Ages, the moral life was understood as a response to the question of happiness, a question posed sharply by the experience of evil and of suffering. All schools of thought accepted this starting point without discussion. They differed among themselves in the responses they gave to this question and, among other things, in the role they afforded to pleasure.

With respect to law, these moralists viewed it as a work of wisdom rather than as a constraint on one's freedom.

From the fourteenth century onward the perspective changes radically. The question of happiness is quickly set aside, and moral analysis increasingly focuses on the obligations imposed by law as the expression of the divine will. The manuals of moral theology no longer contain a treatise on happiness, as St. Thomas had, although he remains their great authority. Consequently, in their view, one can construct an ethics and live a moral life without ever considering the question of happiness. Kant, for his part, critiques what he calls "eudemonism," (from the Greek term eudaimonia: happiness), criticizing any system that introduces into moral intention a consideration of happiness viewed as an end. He maintains that "all eudemonists are practical egoists" and asserts that "to make eudemonism the foundation of virtue is to euthanize morality." He was reacting against utilitarianism, which was just arising in England at the time, and which proposed happiness as the end of moral action, but a happiness that was viewed as the well-being of the greatest number. He wanted to safeguard the excellence of the act of intention by making it a pure obedience to the categorical imperative.

Indeed, isn't this problem present in all of our consciences? Don't we recognize that the moral law often demands that we renounce happiness understood as pleasure, comfort or utility? Don't we sense that concern for happiness runs the risk of introducing into our lives an egotistical fervor capable of vitiating our best intentions?

The Divorce between Happiness and Moral Theology

We can see, therefore, that both in history and in experience a certain divorce has occurred between happiness and morality: Can we be moral without renouncing happiness? Can we be happy without transgressing the demands of morality? The question is crucial, for in fact we can renounce neither happiness nor morality.

This issue spills over, so to speak, into the love that we spontaneously associate with happiness. Shouldn't love also be regulated by law, lest it become a dangerous passion? Consequently, Kant gives priority to duty over love in his interpretation of the first commandment of God. For Kant this commandment imposes a duty and not a sentiment. Similarly, the manuals of moral theology reduce the treatise on charity to an exposition of the obligations tied to this virtue. A critical question results from this: Can one love from duty in order to fulfill an obligation? Or, in order to be moral, must one repress love and bridle its exuberance? Yet, if this is the case, does not the moral law become something that extinguishes love and even threatens charity?

The debate has important consequences for the relationship between moral theology and the Gospel. Does not the Sermon on the Mount begin by presenting us Beatitudes, which, according to the Fathers, are Christ's response to the question of happiness? Does not the Gospel also in many places promise rewards to us? Does this mean that we should reproach certain sayings in the Gospels because they encourage self-interest and support eudemonism?

Thus, our problem looms larger. The divorce between morality and happiness has implications for the relationship between morality and the Gospel. The issue is the following: how to reconcile the moral life with happiness and love, and place it in unrestricted contact with the Gospel?

The Root of the Problem: Freedom for Excellence versus Freedom of Indifference

In our view, the roots of the issue we have just raised reside in two distinct conceptions of freedom that have engendered two types of morality: the *freedom of indifference*, which is the source of moralities of obligation, and *freedom for excellence*, which inspires moralitie. of happiness and the virtues. Let us now make a brief detour that will prove worthwhile for our overall analysis.

Historically, the theory underlying the freedom of indifference arose at the turn of the fourteenth century in the Franciscan school's critique of the thought of Thomas Aquinas, especially the critique advanced by William of Ockham (d. 1349), the initiator of the nominalism that soon spread throughout Europe.

Everything hinges on one's interpretation of the classical definition of free choice (*liberum arbitrium*) formulated in the middle of the twelfth century by Peter Lombard in his *Sentences*.

> Free choice is that faculty of reason and will by which we either choose the good with the assistance of grace, or choose evil without such assistance.
>
> *Sentences*, b. 2, dist. 24, c. 3.

St. Thomas had argued that free choice proceeds from both reason and will. It was thus a power to choose derived from our two spiritual faculties and quickened by the inclinations to truth, goodness, and happiness that animate these faculties. Hence, one can call it a freedom for excellence or perfection. It is the power to engage in excellent actions, actions that are both true and good, even though the agent may in fact fail and do evil.

Ockham squarely reverses the relationship: Free choice does not *proceed* from reason and will; instead, it *precedes* them on the level of action, for we can choose to think or not to think, to will or not to will. Hence, free choice is the first faculty of the human person, whose act does not originally depend on anything but his or her own choice.

It will be defined as the power to choose indifferently between contraries, between yes and no, good and evil. Hence, it is rightly described as a freedom of indifference.

A veritable revolution is occurring here in the conception of the human person and of human action. This revolution begins by breaking away from spiritual nature and its inclinations, especially its inclination to happiness. Ockham affirms that the human person can choose indifferently between being happy and not being happy, as well as between preserving or not preserving his existence. Nature is no longer the source of freedom; it is henceforth subordinated to choice, being below and external to it. The famous maxim of the Ancients, *sequi naturam* (follow nature) loses its meaning; instead, a new vision emerges: *dominari naturam.* The ideal becomes the domination and enslavement of nature. Let us now consider how two profoundly different conceptions of morality spring from these two definitions of freedom. We shall begin by considering the freedom for excellence that was common to the thinkers of Antiquity, whether they were Christians or pagans.

How Freedom for Excellence Engenders Moralities of Happiness

We can compare freedom for excellence with an acquired skill in an art or a profession; it is the capacity to produce our acts when and how we wish, like high-quality works that are perfect in their domain. From our birth we have received moral freedom as a talent to be developed, as a seed containing the knowledge of truth and the inclination toward goodness and happiness, an inclination diversified according to what the Ancients called the *semina virtutum,* the seeds of the virtues. At the beginning of our lives, these capacities are weak, as is the case for a child or an apprentice. Like our personalities, we must form our freedom through an education appropriate to our level of development. This educational process appears to pass through three stages, analogous to the stages of a human life. Corresponding to childhood, there is the apprenticeship of rules and laws of action, during which we learn with the help of our parents and teachers how to live a disciplined life. Next there is the adolescence of the moral life, characterized by increasing independence and growing personal initiative, guided by one's taste for the true and the good and strengthened by one's experience. It is here that virtue begins to emerge as an excellence or capacity for personal action. There then arrives the age of maturity where virtue blossoms like a talent in the arts: It is a daring, intelligent and generous force, the capacity to bring to good completion works of long duration that bear fruit for many; it secures ease and joy in action.

Freedom for excellence engenders a moral science that directly takes up the question of happiness and the absolute good. It is a science that regards the question of happiness as decisive for the integral ordering of one's life and the formation of one's character. This science is organized according to the principal virtues that strengthen freedom and refine human action, without, however, neglecting the examination of the opposing faults, vices, and sins contrary to freedom. This science is brought to completion in the study of law in its educational role, a role that firmly brings together wisdom and love, and even constraint, which is sometimes necessary in the struggle against evil.

This type of freedom is easily open to an encounter with Christian revelation. The natural inclination toward truth and goodness is the work of God. God conforms the human person to the likeness of his wisdom and goodness and, as an interior master, calls him to participate more deeply in his creative freedom. This bond with God is intimate and from birth. It touches the essence of our personality in our longing for happiness and love. It does not limit human freedom, but grounds it. The more one is open to the action of God from a just and sincere heart, the more one sees one's interior freedom blossom, as St. Paul teaches. In this way we can easily recognize in the scriptural narrative the liberating action of God on behalf of his people and of the Holy Spirit in the hearts of all believers. A close collaboration between grace and freedom can be established, above and beyond the inevitable debates due to sin.

The advent of divine revelation has occasioned a profound transformation in the doctrine of virtue. The first source of moral excellence is no longer located in the human person, but in God through Christ. This transformation is evident in the doctrine of "infused" moral virtues, which are not "acquired" by unaided human effort, but implanted in the human person by the Holy Spirit. Nevertheless, the divine source of these infused moral virtues does not make them less personal. They are just as intimate as the theological virtues' acts of believing, hoping, and loving. Nor does their divine source make them less the action of the agent, for they interiorly take up the so-called "human" virtues clustered around the four virtues classically regarded as primary: prudence (or practical wisdom), justice, courage (or fortitude), and temperance (or self-mastery). Thus, in the context of a gradual education guided by the light of the Gospel, an active cooperation between God and the human person can develop. It is a cooperation rooted in faith and love and guided by the Holy Spirit, who intervenes with his gifts like a master craftsman. Properly understood, therefore, a theory of virtue that brings freedom for excellence to perfection has a close affinity with the Scriptures. Some such theory seems necessary if we are to explain what the Scriptures teach concerning the way to live as followers of Christ.

How Freedom of Indifference Engenders Moralities of Obligation

When we consider freedom of indifference, we discover that we are in a new moral universe. It is lodged between two freedoms that confront each other: the freedom of the human person and the freedom of God. No natural bond connects them, for nature is now subordinated to freedom. Nature only establishes an exterior relationship shaped by their differences: The omnipotence of the Creator gives him absolute power over the human person, which he especially exercises by means of the moral law. The moral law expresses the divine will, which is perfectly free and sovereign, while it limits human freedom by commanding or forbidding certain actions with the force of obligation. Law is the source of morality. In fact, human acts, since they are born of a choice between contraries, are by nature indifferent; they become morally good or bad insofar as they conform to a legal obligation. Law itself depends entirely on God. God could, in principle, at the whim of his will, modify any one of the law's precepts. Ockham pushed this view to its logical extreme. Without hesitation he affirmed that if God ordered someone to hate him, in this case hate itself would become good, being an act of obedience to the Creator's will. It would be impossible to express more clearly the view that obedience to law has priority over love.

With the advent of nominalism we witness the formation of the first morality of obligation: the moral life will henceforth be circumscribed by obligations. The desire for happiness will systematically be set aside.

From within this view of morality, what concretely is the moral law? We find it first of all in the Scriptures, inspired by God, especially in the Ten Commandments, understood as a code of moral obligations, and in the conclusions that one can draw from them. Moral precepts are in principle subordinated to the divine free will and to its "absolute power." Yet they retain their permanence and validity in what Ockham calls the "ordinary course" of the things determined by the "ordered power of God." This enables the moralist to continue employing the traditional term "natural law" to describe the moral law.

In this conception of morality, the divine will is evident to us through right reason in the form of moral imperatives. All people know from experience that reason commands or forbids certain actions. More precisely, reason reveals these imperatives to us, but does not supply the reasons for them, since no reasons exist other than the pure divine will itself. Therefore, one should obey such precepts simply because they are commanded, and not because of any motive, such as the utility or pleasure they afford. This view already comes close to expressing the categorical imperative of Kant. Moreover, we can see the outlines of the view that moral imperatives would retain their validity even if God did not exist. Tied at first to the divine free will, morality is on the verge of separating itself from God.

The field of moral theology has been profoundly disrupted. Henceforth it will be filled by a scattering of individual acts passing in succession and without connection, being the disparate products of a freedom that at any moment can attach itself to one contrary or another. There is no longer concern for a general goal that would unite these acts in one same intention: the common good or happiness. We have instead a morality of acts and cases of conscience. Little reference will be made to education

Two Forms of Freedom
Two Types of Morality

Freedom for Excellence	*Freedom of Indifference*
Ability to act with excellence and perfection whenever one wishes.	Ability to choose between contraries.
Proceeds from reason and will and from the natural longing for truth, goodness, and happiness.	Precedes and dominates every natural inclination. Proceeds from the will alone in its "indifferenced" to contraries.
Given in germ, it develops gradually through education until it reaches maturity.	It is entirely present from the beginning and in each act of the moral life.
Unites one's actions in an ordered whole through a finality that ties them together interiorly. The principal end is "happiness" attained through union with the "absolute good."	Each free act is independent of all others. The moral life is a succession of "cases of conscience." Moral theology is a "casuistry" governed by obedience to law.
Virtue is an aspect of freedom. It is the personal ability, whether acquired or infused, to act with perfection. It causes joy.	Virtue is a habit of submission to law.
Law has an educational role in the growth of freedom. It is a work of wisdom and corresponds to one's most intimate longings.	Law is external to freedom, which it limits through obligation. It is the work of the pure will of the legislator.
Engenders a morality of happiness and virtue, which springs from one's interior inclinations.	Engenders a morality of law and obligation. The question of happiness is extrinsic to morality.

or progress because this moral view presupposes a freedom that is wholly given the instant conscience awakes in the soul. It is a freedom that knows no degrees and can be limited only in its external expression. Virtue loses here its formative role and becomes nothing more than a habit.

How to Repair the Divorce between Happiness and the Moral Life

Let us return to our central problem, the divorce between morality and happiness. It would appear that we have a solid explanation for this divorce, rooted both in history and in the internal logic of thought itself. This separation has its origin in the ascendance of the freedom of indifference and its separation from the natural inclinations expressed in the longing for happiness. In this way, the moral life lost the interior source of freedom that had nourished it. Moral theology was now forced to search for a new external source of freedom. In other words, the human person was no longer inherently moral; he or she had to become moral artificially, through the constraint of law, imposed by God, by society, or by pure reason.

This divorce was so deep that it altered the most fundamental notion in moral theology: the conception of the good. In the past, the good and happiness formed a single concept expressed by a single word: goodness, *bonum* in Latin. Happiness was the diffusion of the good, like the reverse side of a single quality. Now, however, defined by its conformity to legal obligation, the good is understood as separated from happiness and even as opposed to it. The desire to be happy appears to endanger the purity of one's intention and to threaten freedom because of the hold happiness continues to retain on the inner life of the human person. It seems as if the morally good person now experiences an almost instinctive fear of happiness.

How can we lessen this divide? How can we achieve a

reconciliation between morality and happiness, both in thought and in experience? By offering us the model for another type of morality, the notion of freedom for excellence shows us the way to respond and offers us the promise of renewal.

Rediscovering Spiritual Nature

The key to renewal is to rediscover our spiritual nature in its spontaneous yearning for truth, goodness, and happiness, flowing from a single primal dynamism. We refer here to "nature" in its original meaning, signifying "from birth." Yet this nature is spiritual, being the image of God's own life. It is part of the very constitution of our personality, as a principle of universality. To renew freedom in its roots requires more of us than merely a discussion of ideas. It is only attainable through the experience of personal action that is true and good; through a humble and patient reflection on this action; as well as through the grace of a quiet light that one must learn to await. It is here, under this intimate flash where the good shines forth, that the desire for happiness is revealed in its best light. By excluding this desire from morality, we have deformed it and painted a false picture of it, because the desire for happiness is itself a spark of the divine image within us. How can we restore the desire for happiness to its primal nature, a nature that was so deeply united to the good that it was itself a sign of moral excellence?

Pleasure and Joy
Two Conceptions of Happiness

We offer here a principle of renewal that is within everyone's grasp. The concerns that make one suspicious of the desire for happiness are the following: It is an individual, self-interested, and easily egoistic feeling; it is contrary to disinterested love, to self-forgetfulness, and to the generosity we normally attribute to moral worth, which demands of us a sense of duty; if we let it enter into the moral life, the primary focus will become the search for personal comfort or utility, for one's individual good in opposition to the universality of moral norms. Therefore, shouldn't we classify systems that make happiness the criterion of moral judgment as "utilitarian" or even as "hedonistic"? The primacy of sense experience is what underlies each of these concerns.

Now, when one reads attentively the authors, especially the Christian authors, who regarded the moral life as a search for happiness, one perceives first of all that they were perfectly aware of the problem. Their first concern was to address the issue of pleasure as a primal human experience and to take a position concerning it, in marked contrast to modern moralists, who in general scarcely address the issue.

But the key feature to recognize is that the best definitions of happiness offered by the authors of the older view go beyond pleasure and ground happiness in the experience of joy, something that is quite different from pleasure. St. Augustine bears witness to this in his *Confessions* (bk. 10, nn. 21–23). The bishop of Hippo begins by presenting the question of happiness itself in terms of joy.

> Thus all agree that they want to be happy, just as
> they would, if questioned, all agree that they want
> to rejoice, and it is joy itself that they call the
> happy life.

Augustine then offers his famous definition of happiness that has become classic: "The happy life is joy born of the truth (*gaudium de veritate*)." He explains this magnificently, addressing himself directly to God:

> But for those who freely serve you, for them, you
> are their joy. And this is the happy life, this alone,
> to rejoice in you, from you, through you.

The Evangelical Beatitudes likewise culminate, after the purifications they engender, in the invitation to enter the joy reserved for those persecuted for the name of Christ. Clearly, this is not an invitation to pleasure.

We are dealing here with two profoundly different experiences, pleasure and joy, which underlie two distinct conceptions of happiness: One belongs to the domain of the senses; the other belongs directly to the moral and spiritual level. Let us note their essential differences: Pleasure is an agreeable sensation, a passion caused by contact with some *exterior* good. Joy, however, is something *interior*, like the act that causes it. Joy is the direct effect of an *excellent action*, like the savor of a long task finally accomplished. It is also the effect in us of truth understood and goodness loved. Thus, we associate joy with virtue, regarding it as a sign of virtue's authenticity.

Pleasure is *opposed to pain* as its contrary. The two are essentially incompatible. Joy, on the other hand, is *born of trials*, of pains endured, of sufferings accepted with courage and with love. Pleasure is *brief*, variable and superficial, like the contact that causes it. Joy is *lasting*, like the excellence, the virtues, that engender it. Sense pleasure is *individual*, like sensation itself. It decreases when the good that causes it is divided up and shared more widely; it ceases altogether when this good is absent. Joy is communicable; it grows by being shared and repays sacrifices freely embraced. Joy belongs to the purity and generosity of love.

How Joy Can Reconcile Happiness and the Moral Life
The Scriptures confirm this perspective. New Testament refers to joy in frequent and varied ways. The theme of joy is present everywhere; it virtually erupts in the letter to the *Philippians* (4.4): "Rejoice in the Lord always. I say it again, rejoice!" Joy is a dominant feature of the early Christian consciousness. On the other hand, one rarely finds the

> Nature warns us by a clear sign that our destination is attained. That sign is joy. I mean joy, not pleasure. Pleasure is only a contrivance devised by nature to obtain for the creature the preservation of its life, it does not indicate the direction in which life is thrusting. But joy always announces that life has succeeded, gained ground, conquered. All great joy has a triumphant note. Now, if we take this indication into account and follow this new line of facts, we find that wherever there is joy, there is creation; the richer the creation, the deeper the joy.
>
> Henri Bergson
> *Mind-Energy: Lectures and Essays*
> (New York: Holt and Company, 1920), p. 29

term *hédonè*: pleasure. The sacred authors either avoid it or they employ it in a pejorative sense, as in the parable of the sower, where wealth and pleasures, like thorns, choke the good seed (Lk 8.4–8, 11–15).

Without doubt, we should not exaggerate the separation between pleasure and joy, for they can coexist and interact with each other. Yet we should clearly distinguish the specific experiences that they generate if we wish to discover the true nature of our inclination to happiness. We cannot enclose this type of desire within the confines of sensible experience, for it belongs to the level of our mind and heart, where deep within us we encounter the yearning for truth, goodness, and love that constitutes the moral order. Indeed, how could one separate joy from the search for truth, the struggle toward the good, and the motions of love, without extinguishing its spiritual vitality?

Thus, the experience of joy engenders a eudemonism, if we wish to retain the term, entirely different from the one that merited Kant's critique. Joy is perfectly compatible with moral excellence; it is a sign of this excellence and contributes to its perfection. The fount of joy lies in the inner depths of our being, at the roots of our freedom, when this freedom is open to the outpourings of goodness and love.

Yet, in order for the waters of this fount to pour forth within us, we have to make a personal choice of great price: When we receive the call to a greater good, a good that will reveal to us the true joy at the core of our lives, will we know how to break free from the charms of pleasure through a liberating renunciation? The discovery of joy beyond our trials is a decisive step on the way to moral maturity. One even comes to perceive, upon fulfilling its requirements, that joy does not destroy, but rather refines and rightly orders, pleasure.

Starting from this experience, we can reestablish the vital bond that unites joy to the virtues, which have become so anemic and lackluster in the moralities of obligation. We can also understand how the virtues are like the arteries that carry strength and disperse joy throughout the entire organism of the moral life.

The reconciliation of morality and happiness by

> By this is my Father glorified, that you bear much fruit and become my disciples. As the Father loves me, so also I love you. Remain in my love. If you keep my commandments, you will remain in my love, just as I have kept my Father's commandments and remain in his love. I have told you this so that my joy may be in you and your joy may be complete.
>
> *John* 15.8–11

means of joy is, in my view, an essential condition for the renewal of moral theology. To establish this reconciliation firmly, we must even revise our understanding of freedom by rediscovering our spiritual nature. On this foundation we can begin the restoration of Christian morality. We shall pursue two trajectories in this labor: We shall strive to reinsert the action of the Holy Spirit into the moral life in harmony with the Evangelical Law, and we shall attempt to strengthen the doctrine of the natural law from the perspective of our natural inclinations.

VII

The Holy Spirit and the New Law

We can justly deplore the absence of the Holy Spirit in Catholic moral theology during the past few centuries. The action of the Holy Spirit was reserved for the spiritual life, understood as something outside the domain of moral theology, or pigeonholed as belonging to mysticism. From this perspective, it became practically impossible to show how the Holy Spirit acts in the life of every Christian from the moment of our Baptism and intervenes in our moral actions.

The conception of freedom for excellence that we have presented offers us the necessary foundation for restoring to the Christian life its tenor as a "life in the Spirit," in line with the teachings of St. Paul and the desires of the Second Vatican Council. It shows us how moral action flows from within the human person, like a spring nourished by our yearnings for truth, goodness, and happiness. Indeed, this is how the Spirit acts. Even if in the arts or in the realm of ideas, our inspirations seem to come to us from on high, we are still aware that these inspirations move us from within and become ours as we act upon them. Similarly, although the motion of the Holy Spirit flows from a source higher than ourselves, it touches us intimately, moving us to engage in a personal act. This is why the Scriptures particularly attribute to the Spirit the motion of love, an attribution that best reveals what this active communion can be. Yet, by severing freedom from our natural inclinations and by placing the origin of the moral life in an external law, the theory of freedom of indifference breaks the lines of communication between the action of the Spirit, morality, and law. The rupture does not remain merely on the level of ideas; it penetrates the depths of our moral conscience.

The New or Evangelical Law

We shall describe how the Holy Spirit acts in the life of the Christian by turning to the analysis of the New or Evangelical Law that St. Thomas offers at the end of his study of law (ST I-II 106–8). We find there a remarkable theological formulation of the spiritual renewal that was occurring in the thirteenth century, a renewal expressed in the evangelical concerns of that age and embodied in the lives of St. Francis and St. Dominic. Thomas' teaching is nourished directly by St. Matthew, St. Paul, and the most beautiful passages of the Prophets. Unfortunately, over the course of the centuries, this treatise has been almost completely forgotten; moralists are just now in the process of recovering it.

The various elements of the definition of the New Law are the following. It is an interior or infused law. It consists in the grace of the Holy Spirit, received through faith in Christ and operating through charity. This is its primary element and the source of its dynamism and power. This law also contains secondary external elements: It has as its concrete text the Sermon on the Mount, and as its instruments the sacraments. This is its matter.

The Spiritual Elements of the New Law

Let us consider each of these elements. The notion that the Evangelical Law is an interior law was a novel view in St. Thomas' day and continues to be so in our own. Isn't

The New Law
Is it a Written Law?

The New Law is the law of the New Testament. But the law of the New Testament is infused in our hearts, for the Apostle says (*Heb* 8.10), quoting the authority of Jeremiah (31.31): "the days are coming, says the Lord, when I will make a new covenant with the house of Israel and the house of Judah," and explaining what this testament is, he adds: "this is the covenant I will establish with the house of Israel. . . . I will put my laws in their minds and I will write them upon their hearts." Therefore the New Law is infused.

I answer that "each thing appears to be what is most prominent in it," as the Philosopher states (*Nicomachean Ethics* 9.8). Now, that which is most prominent in the law of the New Testament, and in which all its power resides, is the grace of the Holy Spirit, which is given through faith in Christ. Consequently the New Law is chiefly the grace itself of the Holy Spirit, which is given to Christ's faithful. This is clear from what the Apostle says (*Rom* 3.27): "Where is . . . your boasting? It is excluded. By what law? Of works? No, but by the law of faith"; for he calls the grace itself of faith "a law." And still more clearly he states (*Rom* 8.2): "The law of the spirit of life in Christ Jesus has delivered me from the law of sin and death." Hence, Augustine says (*On the Spirit and the Letter* 24) that "as the law of deeds was inscribed on tablets of stone, so the law of faith is inscribed on the hearts of the faithful," and elsewhere in the same book (21): "What else are the divine laws inscribed by God himself on our hearts, but the very presence of the Holy Spirit?"

Nevertheless the New Law contains certain things that dispose us to receive the grace of the Holy Spirit, and pertain to the use of that grace. These things are secondary, so to speak, in the New Law; the faithful needed to be instructed concerning them, both by word and by writing, about what they should believe, as well as what they should do. Consequently we must say that the New Law is primarily an infused law, but secondarily a written law.

St. Thomas Aquinas
Summa theologiae I-II 106.1

the Gospel written and preached, and thus something external, brought to us from outside? Moreover, how can we associate law with interiority? Aren't they contraries?

An Interior Law

The work of the Holy Spirit is to enter within us by touching the two deepest cords of our hearts, the affinity for truth and the yearning for goodness and happiness. The Spirit acts through a quiet light and a gentle motion that produce in our souls wisdom and love. This interior motion is the marrow, so to speak, of the New Law. It is what the prophet long ago had already announced: "I will place my law within them, and write it upon their hearts" (*Jer* 31.33). Christian experience confirms this when it calls the Holy Spirit the Interior Master: he enlightens us concerning the Word we have heard and moves us to live it with sincerity.

Clearly the term "law" acquires here a new meaning, far removed from any juridicism; it is a deepening and a spiritual enrichment of the concept. The New Law is close to the natural law, whose roots are likewise internal. The New Law also becomes the rule of the love infused by the Spirit. After all, are not these terms at the service of reality and experience?

The Root: Faith in Christ

Faith in Christ marks the starting point of the New Law within us. We have too frequently forgotten that faith in Christ is the mother of Christian morality; we have reduced faith to a few obligations concerning truths to be believed under the pain of sin, and have attenuated the lines that link faith to works. When St. Paul in the letter to the *Romans* encounters Jewish morality, stiffened in its justice according to observances of the Law, and Greek morality, draped in its pretensions to wisdom, he boldly confronts them with faith in the crucified Christ, who has become for us the wisdom and justice of God. This is the source of the moral life according to the Gospel; it depends on the Holy Spirit, who enkindles faith and teaches from within the wisdom and justice of God.

The advent of faith effects an original and substantial transformation in the moral life. It centers the moral life on a particular person: Jesus, the Christ. In his historical particularity – in his body that suffered and was resurrected – Jesus becomes the source and cause of justice and wisdom. In short, he becomes the source and cause of moral excellence for those who believe in him. Jesus is not merely a sage or a model. By means of the personal ties that faith and love initiate, he establishes such a close spiritual communion between himself and his disciples that St. Paul will present the Christian life as "life in Christ." He even affirms that, "It is no longer I who live, but Christ who lives in me" (*Gal* 2.20). This view is unique among the moralities and religions of the world: For Christians, the person of Jesus has become the center of the moral life, as he is also the center of prayer and the liturgy that nourishes it.

It is appropriate to note that it is here that faith acquires its full force. Faith does not signify, as it often does today, merely a certain opinion about life or a mental adherence to a creed. Faith is a vital act; it commits one person to another forever. In this way, marriage is rooted in an act of faith between spouses who are bound together in their love. This act entails some understanding of their common future, an understanding that is, in a sense, prophetic. Similarly, every fruitful decision, whether on the personal, political, or even artistic level, flows from an act of faith in a "certain idea" that inspires and guides the work to its completion. No science, properly understood, can produce the intuition of faith; it is a knowledge belonging to a different order. Tied to life and love in their vitality, faith becomes the interior rule guiding one's creative and constructive actions. It engenders hope, which gives life its energy. Faith in Christ, therefore, is like an interior law for building up the moral life of the Christian.

The Sap of the Tree: Charity

"Working through charity" (*Gal* 5.6). If faith is like the root, charity is like the sap that nourishes the trunk and rises into the branches, the network of virtues, to produce the delicious fruit of good works. It is through this new love revealed and shared in Christ that the Holy Spirit works in us. The primacy of charity among the gifts and the virtues is clearly taught by St. Paul in *1 Corinthians* (chs. 12 and 13) and by St. John, who makes it a new commandment (*Jn* 13.34). This teaching is rich. Because of its force and universality, which extends even to enemies, we can call this teaching specifically Christian. As the doctrine unfolds, it reveals how charity animates all the virtues.

Charity and the Virtues

Charity is commonly described as the mother and form of the virtues. It generates and inspires their organic unity, which theology regards as clustered around the theological and cardinal virtues. The virtues are interconnected, acting and growing together like the members of a living body. We should note, however, that while Christian authors have embraced the philosophers' conception of the virtues, they profoundly transform this conception, precisely because of their experience of charity. The virtue of the philosophers, no matter how elevated and open it may be, leaves the human person alone in his efforts, always tempted to enclose himself in his own excellence. The infusion of love into the roots of the virtues effects a vital transformation: By placing us in communion with the person of Christ, charity renders us so receptive to the motion of his Spirit that we can no longer regard our virtues as our own property. Although they remain something deeply personal within us, they have become the property of the one who now inspires them. An interior attitude characteristic of love results from this: an active receptivity, a dynamic welcoming, a cheerful and willing obedience to the Spirit that engenders an action all the stronger for no longer being the action of one person alone. Through charity, this attitude, uniting docility with initiative, is conveyed to the other virtues and marks their actions.

Charity and the Gifts of the Holy Spirit

In an effort to offer a more satisfying account of this particular experience, St. Thomas follows St. Augustine and develops his theology of the gifts. In conjunction with the virtues, the gifts make us receptive to the impulses of the Spirit of Christ. The list of seven gifts is taken from Isaiah (11.1–8, as they appear in the Greek *Septuagint*). They are *wisdom, understanding, counsel, courage, knowledge, piety*, and *fear of the Lord*. The gifts give our acts a higher vitality and perfection. As we have seen, St. Thomas relates a gift to each of the virtues. In this way, the virtues and gifts form the twin visage of one and the same organism of love that underlies the works of the Holy Spirit in the lives of the faithful.

The involvement of the Holy Spirit in our growth in virtue shows us that the Spirit acts in us through the normal paths of daily effort, rather than through extraordinary revelations, sudden motions, or exceptional charisms. He moves us like sap, whose movement we neither see nor sense, so discrete is he before the activities and projects that engross us. Yet his gradual push, along with our confident fidelity, prepares the way for the flowering of spring and the growth of autumn. The Spirit, therefore, can produce in us works that are sometimes quite surprising. Unfolding within us as deep inspirations, the gifts can move us beyond the simple measure of reason in the use of goods, and in acts of generosity, courage, and detachment. St. Francis of Assisi, for example, became the lover of Lady Poverty; St. Vincent de Paul and Mother Teresa were devoted to the destitute. There are also martyrs such as St. Cyprian at Carthage and the humble Blandina at Lyons, who, following the model of Stephen in the *Acts of the Apostles*, retained a peaceful, even joyous confidence in the face of torments and death. In this way, the gifts lead the virtues to their perfection.

The Material Elements of the New Law
In a beautiful text inspired by the prologue of the Gospel of John, St. Thomas completes his teaching on the New Law by showing us how the grace of the Holy Spirit comes to us from the Son of God made man. He then shows how the New Law contains the other spiritual elements mentioned earlier: certain sensible realities that in some fashion incarnate this grace in order to convey it to us, as well as certain concrete acts that give us a share in his own labors. No matter how intellectual we are, we are not pure spirits. To receive the Word of God, we need tangible signs. The Word comes to us through our eyes and ears, by what is written and preached. We must also put this Word into practice in our own day. The Son of God walked this path in a surprising way, through the incarnation and the cross. The grace of the Spirit likewise comes to us through material realities: through books, like the Bible whose moral teaching culminates in the Sermon on the Mount; through sacred objects and chosen actions: these are the sacraments and the liturgy that surrounds them (*ST* I-II 108.1).

The Sermon on the Mount
Text of the New Law

Endowed with the authority of the Lord, the Sermon on the Mount was considered by the Fathers as the principal source of moral instruction; the Sermon has directly inspired most movements of spiritual renewal in the Church. St. Thomas, therefore, does not hesitate to present it as the specific text of the New Law, analogous to the Ten Commandments for the Old Law.

The Sermon, however, should not be considered in isolation. It is the summit and point of convergence of the moral teaching of the Scriptures, and of the New Testament in particular. We must interpret it, therefore, in relation to whole of the Scriptures of which it is a part. Nor does the Sermon address only personal morality. Like the Gospels, the Sermon speaks to the ecclesial community it helps form. Thus, we can say that the Sermon on the Mount gives the Church its fundamental constitution: It provides the underlying basis of ecclesiastical legislation, as well as of the rules and constitutions that religious communities have developed over the course of history.

Nevertheless, the Sermon is not like other legal texts precisely because it is the instrument of the Holy Spirit in the work of justification and sanctification. Taken only on the material level, the text of the Sermon certainly can no more justify and sanctify a person than the Ten Commandments can. Perhaps it is even less apt in this regard because its demands are so great that they can appear impossible to fulfill. Yet, when the grace of the Spirit of Christ intervenes, with faith and love, the Sermon on the Mount becomes a choice instrument for such work: It describes, at the heart of Christian experience, the paths of spiritual liberation. Animated in this way, it truly merits being called "the law of freedom."

We can find three reasons for justifying St. Thomas' practice of calling the Evangelical Law, the law of freedom.

1. *The Sermon on the Mount does not add any material prescriptions to the precepts of the Ten Commandments.* Instead, viewed from the context of the Gospel, it frees us from the multiple external observances of the Jewish law, retaining only the essential moral precepts. This allows us to concentrate our efforts and attention on the level of the "heart," where, in loving faith, the virtues are formed and blossom. Through this moderation and flexibility, the Sermon prepares and promotes spiritual growth.

2. *The Sermon on the Mount leads us into a new order of things.* Law normally established between people relationships of master to servant. Law was expressed in the imperative, and it sanctioned predetermined penalties. The New Law establishes us in relationships of friendship with the Lord, according to his word:

> I no longer call you servants, because a servant does not know what his master is doing. I call you friends, because I have told you everything I have heard from my Father (*Jn* 15.15).

In friendship, imperatives and commands are no longer appropriate. Friends interact on a more personal level, through exhortation (as in the apostolic *paraclesis*) or by offering counsel. The New Law differs from other laws precisely because it adds counsels to its precepts. These counsels call for our personal initiative, something which the virtues and the gifts best prepare us to undertake. The goal of the Sermon, therefore, is to teach us how to live our spiritual freedom in the context of our friendship with the Lord and with our brothers and sisters that charity forms within us. St. Paul refers to the freedom of the children of God, distinguishing it from the status of slaves or underage children in the house of the Father (*Rom* 8.14–17; *Gal* 4.1–7).

The evangelical counsels are addressed to all Christians, to each one according to his particular situation and vocation. They will later be condensed into the three vows of poverty, chastity, and obedience that are the underpinnings of religious life, ordered to the perfection of charity and to bearing witness to the Gospel throughout the Church.

3. *One cannot fulfill the Sermon on the Mount from constraint, from obligation or from duty. It is only attainable through the way of love, which rests at the center of its teaching and is the first gift of the Spirit.* This love makes us free because it makes us act of our own accord, by our own inclination and spiritual enjoyment, in imitation of Christ and according to the preferences of the Spirit. We cannot, however, enjoy or exercise such freedom unless we have accepted the detachments and purifications that are necessary in order to learn true love and be freed from our selfish instincts. This is the work of the Beatitudes, which lead us from poverty and humility to purity and peace in hearts that have become entirely receptive to the action of the Spirit.

The Sacraments, Instruments of the New Law

The sacraments are the second material element of the New Law. They are a necessary part of a moral theology that gives the grace of Christ an essential role in the moral life. This grace gives us inner strength and establishes us in a vital union with the Lord, a union expressed in the analogies of the body and its members, the vine and its branches. The sacraments are instruments of the Holy Spirit that communicate this grace to us through words and gestures, sensible and expressive signs, such as the water of Baptism, the bread and wine of the Eucharist, the anointing with oil and the imposition of hands. The Church has placed the celebration of the sacraments in a liturgy centered on the Lord's passion and resurrection, of which the Eucharist is the "memorial." The Church has also structured the seasons of the year to reproduce in the lives of the faithful the principal stages or "mysteries" in the work of Christ. For the Christian, the liturgy, which is the highest form of prayer, maintains close ties with the moral life. The Church's constant use of the moral and spiritual texts of the New Testament in its ceremonies points to these close ties. According to St. Paul, the moral life is a form of spiritual worship. It generates in the lives of each person what the eucharistic liturgy signifies (*Rom* 12.1).

Ecclesial Institutions at the service of the New Law

Lastly, we can apply our definition of the New Law to institutions in the Church, and show how we cannot set them in opposition to the action of the Holy Spirit because these institutions are also his instruments. Although moral action is quite personal, since it is animated by the faith and love of Christ, it always has an ecclesial dimension. It is always necessarily integrated into the life of the Church, understood as the "Body of Christ" animated by the Spirit. St. Paul always locates his moral teaching within this framework, understood in a vital and realistic way. Like the New Law itself, this communion of life and action is principally something spiritual; yet, it must be incarnated in external visible realities. The institutions of the Church are realities of this type: the ecclesiastical hierarchy, community organizations at all levels, the regulations of canon law, and so forth. These have developed over the course of history from evangelical seeds and provide support for the Church's action.

Institutions in the Church pose certain problems,

depending on the use that one makes of them. They become dangerous when we treat them, by analogy with merely human institutions, as vehicles for personal ambition, special interests or orchestrated domination. The Gospel is emphatic about this, as the words of Jesus to his Apostles testify:

> You know that the rulers of the Gentiles lord it over them, and the great ones make their authority over them felt. But it shall not be so among you. Rather, whoever wishes to be great among you shall be your servant; whoever wishes to be first among you shall be your slave. For the Son of Man did not come to be served but to serve and to give his life as a ransom for many (*Mt* 20.25–28).

This is the interior revolution that the grace of Christ works within us. It teaches us to employ institutions and exercise authority in a spirit of service, with unselfishness and generosity, imitating the "service" of Christ who gave his life "for many." Indeed, when we are devoted to a position of authority that has been entrusted to us, we develop a cluster of different virtues: care for the common good; attention to the needs of each person; discernment about what is appropriate; courage and perseverance in carrying out decisions; fraternal patience and forgiveness in the face of criticism; unselfishness in serving a project that does not interest or pertain to us. Pastoral ministry is one of the consummate forms of fraternal charity and a very instructive school of moral experience.

The doctrine of the New Law, therefore, enables us to present all the dimensions of Christian morality and to order its many diverse elements. It directs a life that is both personal and ecclesial. It is both profoundly spiritual and incarnational. It unites the Spirit to the letter of the

Gospel, faith to the sacraments, interior prayer to the unfolding of the liturgy. It links the breath of the Spirit to the management of institutions and the application of law. Such a work cannot be done without the aid of the Holy Spirit; without living faith; without vigorous and prayerful charity; nor without the support of ecclesial communion. The promises, however, are present, written in the Scriptures and in our hearts.

VIII

Natural Law and Freedom

We have considered the Christian moral life from the perspective of what comes to it from above, from the Holy Spirit. Now we shall consider its relationship to human nature.

Is the Natural Law Internal or External to Us?

We have seen how the freedom of indifference creates a radical opposition between nature and free will. In a certain sense, this causes the natural law to be expelled from freedom. While it had traditionally been considered as the first foundation of the moral life, the natural law is now placed in opposition to freedom, as an external limit imposed on it by the nature of things. Yet the natural law was also attacked from behind by this same freedom because like all law it was placed under the arbitrary will of God. Consequently, the natural law now offered morality a precarious foundation, like an ice bridge over an abyss. In an effort to lessen this radical relativism underlying nominalist thought, moralists did their best to reinforce the indispensable natural foundation of morality by grounding it in reason. Yet they did not succeed in resolving the opposition between nature and freedom because it merely reappeared in relation to reason. They continued to affirm that the natural law is an interior law, but they considered it as exterior to freedom, often viewing it as merely a biological law, as in the case of sexuality.

This also generates the view that morality itself is something external to us: We are not inherently moral. We become moral under the pressure of a law dictated by God, by the Church, or by society and its customs. Morality becomes a necessary artifact of social life. One can personally internalize it, but it will vary according to the whims of different ages and cultures. It will even depend on civil legislation and the decisions of the majority.

This is a gravely important issue because it touches the foundation of the human rights we strive to enforce today in our efforts to establish a minimum of ethical and juridical consensus throughout the world. Nature does not exist without interiority. The term "nature" signifies the cause of birth, the source of life in the heart of interiority. The tragedy of the freedom of indifference is that it turns away from spiritual interiority and from the life that flows from it as a vital yearning for truth, goodness, and happiness. Has not the time come for us to recover the spiritual roots that remain in the depths of our consciences, below the foment of our intellects?

The perspective of the freedom for excellence shows us the path to follow to return to the intimate springs that water the human mind and heart. These are our natural inclinations or yearnings. They are like a primal spontaneity that we can discern in the intuitive flashes of our minds or in the original vitality of our loves. This rediscovery is fundamentally important. It enables us to understand how morality and the natural law have roots at the foundation of our freedom. It also enables us to grasp that the natural law does not primarily function by constraint, but by attraction. Lastly, it allows us see that the natural law is a vital law that governs the dynamism and development of our faculties of action, rendering them fruitful.

The Five Inclinations that Establish the Natural Law within Us

We shall examine the natural inclinations that nourish our

freedom through the framework that St. Thomas provides when he considers the precepts of the natural law (*ST* I-II 94.2). Thomas' perspective is already substantially present in Cicero in a text that Thomas seems never to have read (*De officiis* 1.4). We can identify five fundamental inclinations. They flow from the essential components of our nature and are linked to the general notions that the philosophers call the "transcendentals" or the "universal attributes." The first inclination at the origin of all human action is (1) the yearning for the good. As we have seen, the yearning for the good is inseparable from the desire for happiness. This inclination becomes known on the intellectual level through the notion of the good, understood as the fullness of perfection, which arises in the experience of Goodness. It gathers the other inclinations into one dynamic stream.

Under the agency of our yearning for the good there next follows (2) the inclination to preserve one's being, an inclination as fundamental as existence itself. It becomes known through the knowledge and experience of being in its existential primacy. It places us in communion with all beings.

Humans are living beings and they have (3) the power to transmit life through the exercise of their sexuality. The human race is divided into male and female for the generation and education of children, a truth expressed both in our consciousness and in our language. On this level we are in communion with all living creatures on the earth.

The fourth inclination is fundamentally spiritual. It is (4) the yearning for truth that becomes known in the notion of the true, as the proper object of the intellect in its theoretical and practical activities. This inclination places us in communion with all other intellectual creatures.

Lastly (5), the human person has a natural inclination

to life in society, an inclination that flows from our awareness of the other, an awareness that is constitutive of our personal being and our awareness of the good. It engenders the desire for communication and communion and is revealed in the gift of language. We shall briefly consider each of these inclinations to show how they ground the natural law and its different precepts, inscribing them at the very heart of our free personality.

1. The Natural Inclination to the Good

The inclination for the good is a primitive spiritual instinct and, as such, is indefinable. One can describe it in terms of what it causes within us: the spontaneous attraction and taste for the good, as well as a repulsion from evil, or more precisely, an attraction and repulsion according to our perception of how things are, according to our reason and our conscience.

The good is more than a duty. It signifies a quality, a perfection that attracts and causes our love. When the good is absent, it incites desire and a movement toward it, as toward an end. When it is present, it causes joy and happiness. The good is lovable and desirable.

The choice between good and evil springs from this attraction because being limited of mind and heart we can choose as good what is really evil, or regard as evil what is truly good. Thus, we can prefer an immorally acquired wealth over the requirements of justice. Since the loved object conforms us to itself, our moral judgment can become distorted and our tastes can become disordered. Yet, underneath the agent's faulty judgments and corrupt loves, the sense of good and evil remains, just as the desire for health remains throughout a sickness.

The attraction of the good is universally expressed in the first principle of morality: Good is to be done and evil avoided. This principle does not primarily signify an obligation to do the good. Rather, it expresses the attraction of the good, which it extends by enjoining us to search for the true good and avoid real evil, beyond the appearances and illusions that confront us. It is this urgency of the truth within the good, within the very attraction of the good, that is at the heart of the intimate awareness of duty and obligation. This awareness, however, does not reduce attraction of the good merely to a duty and an obligation, for it goes beyond them toward the perfection of the good.

The good is tied to love by being its direct cause. Consequently, we can distinguish the species of good according to the species of love or friendship. There is first the pleasurable good, sought for the sensate enjoyment it causes. Then there is the useful good, valued as a means to a proposed end. These two types of good pertain to the love of "concupiscence," in which the agent above all orders to himself the good he desires. This is the case, according to Aristotle, in friendships among the young, which are founded on pleasure and emotion. It also occurs in friendships between merchants and business people, which are based on common utility.

The good in the full sense of the term differs from this. Good most fully signifies that which merits being loved for itself and in itself, as an end and not as a means. Likewise, properly speaking, love consists in loving someone for himself and as he truly is. This is the love of friendship or benevolence. The object of this love is a person or a good that is an aspect of that person's excellence, such as truth, goodness, rectitude, and all true virtue. With this class of goodness and love we fully enter the moral realm.

The inclination toward the good is expressed in the Ten Commandments through the two commandments to love God and neighbor that express the entire law. This inclination lays the foundation for the rights and duties that the other inclinations delineate. In short, the inclination

The Ten Commandments in Catholic Catechesis

1. YOU SHALL LOVE AND ADORE THE ONE GOD COMPLETELY. I am your God, who freed you; you shall not have other gods besides me.

2. YOU SHALL RESPECT HIS HOLY NAME, FLEEING BLASPHEMY AND SWEARING. The name of God is holy; you shall not use it in vain.

3. YOU SHALL KEEP HOLY THE DAY OF THE LORD, SERVING GOD DEVOTEDLY. Each Sunday we celebrate the Lord's Easter mystery.

4. YOU SHALL HONOR YOUR FATHER AND MOTHER, AND ALSO YOUR SUPERIORS. "Honor your father and mother, as the Lord has commanded you" (*Dt* 5.16).

5. YOU SHALL SHUN MURDER, SCANDAL, HATRED AND ANGER. You shall not kill; you shall respect human life.

6. YOU SHALL GUARD PURITY IN ALL YOUR ACTS. You shall not commit adultery; you shall love faithfully.

7. YOU SHALL NOT TAKE NOR HOLD UNJUSTLY THE GOODS OF ANOTHER. You shall not enslave or manipulate another; you shall ensure his freedom and dignity.

8. YOU SHALL BANISH LIES AND SLANDER. May your testimony be true; say what is good about your neighbor.

9. YOU SHALL REMAIN PURE IN YOUR THOUGHTS AND DESIRES. May your love's desires be entirely pure.

10. YOU SHALL NOT COVET THE GOODS OF ANOTHER, SEEKING TO ACQUIRE THEM DISHONESTLY. Look upon your neighbor without desiring his possessions; think of what you can share with him.

The Bishops of Belgium
Livre de la foi

toward the good gives each person the right and instills in him the duty to search for the good and reject and combat what is evil. By activating in concrete actions the general desire for justice and friendship, the virtues develop our inclination toward the good. Love of the good, being simultaneously universal and specific, provides charity its natural foundation. Charity perfects and renews this foundation, subjecting it to the trial of many purifications. Just as we appreciate health better when we are sick, so too we become sensitive to our inclination to the good when we are confronted with evil and suffering, especially when we become aware of our own sin, if this sin has not blinded us. Yet the joy that surpasses this pain is also revelatory.

2. The Natural Inclination to Preserve Being

The inclination to preserve being is fundamental. It touches our very substance, the conservation of our existence and the life that underlies all of our actions. It engenders the desire to exist and the love of health. It gives us a sense of reality and establishes our right to legitimate self-defense.

This inclination, however, is not solely directed toward conservation. It is also dynamic. It pushes us toward what fosters our thriving: toward food, clothing, housing, and so forth. It underlies and promotes the progress and development of our being. This inclination does not pertain solely to our physical life. It also engages the spiritual level: It engenders the natural love of self that underlies all our actions, and is antecedent to any selfish introversion. In this way, this inclination provides the measure of one's love of neighbor in the second commandment ("You shall love your neighbor as yourself" [Mt 22.39]), and is the foundation of the Golden Rule. In order to protect a moral value, such as the love of God, the love of one's country or the love of justice, this inclination can even lead us to sacrifice our physical life.

The inclination to preserve being is expressed in the fifth commandment ("You shall not kill"), which inculcates respect for the life of another, extended also to inculcate respect for his goods. It founds the right to protect one's life and to obtain whatever is necessary to ensure a fitting existence. It also imposes on each of us, as a natural obligation, that we care for our physical and moral health.

This inclination is manifest in the hope that the virtue of courage strengthens when confronting the difficult trials of life. The Christian virtue of hope crowns this vital natural inclination by giving us the gift of divine help in the attainment of promises that surpass all human hope. The journey to such "hope against hope," however, does not occur without a deep trial, analogous to the sacrifice of Abraham that becomes the model of hoping against hope.

The problems of suicide (the yearning for nothingness is like a sickness and a rupture at the heart of the inclination to preserve being), abortion, torture, mutilation, and euthanasia are all located in the domain of this inclination. The inclination to preserve being also underlies the advances in medicine and healthcare that play such an important role in our societies.

3. The Inclination to Marry

Sexual inclination is something that humans share in common with all living beings, but it exists in humans in a more perfect way. It comes to fulfillment in marriage, which unites a man and a women for life. It is not solely biological, even though this component is a characteristic feature of it. It engages the entire personality through the bonds of affection. We commonly distinguish two ends of marriage: first there is generation – the gift of life and the education of children, who ensure the growth and continuance of the human species and its cultural heritage. Second, there is the love and mutual support of the couple. The two finalities naturally aid each other. One cannot be fulfilled without the other, for the law of love is gift and fecundity.

It is also clear that the other inclinations develop within the context of the family. The family is where the first experiences of life occur. It is where we learn about love and happiness, make our first concrete judgments concerning good and evil, and receive our first moral education. The family is where we acquire a sense of existence and confidence in life. It is where we make our first cognitive discoveries and learn our mother tongue; where we discover the differences between the sexes and between personalities. Its diversity of relationships makes the family the model and primary unit of society.

The sexual inclination must be regulated if it is to develop rightly. Three of the Ten Commandments address it: the fourth, which prescribes respect for one's parents; the sixth, which ties intercourse to marriage; the ninth, which forbids lust. These precepts are at the service of chastity, which is one of the forms of temperance or self-mastery over instincts and feelings. If chastity has the negative connotation of struggle against the excesses and deviations of one's sexuality, it is also a deeply positive virtue: It acts in the service of love, contributing to its purity, rectitude, and duration.

This inclination instills in each person a natural right to marry and a corresponding duty to embrace the responsibilities toward one's spouse and children that come with marriage. Christianity, from the very beginning, has grafted onto this inclination the sanctification of marriage and the call to virginity addressed to some. The call to virginity is not a rejection nor a disdaining of marriage, but a witness and special consecration to the love of Christ, a consecrated witness lived in many diverse ways according to the vast diversity of vocations in the Church. Christian chastity is the special work of the Holy Spirit, inspiring a new love in the hearts of the faithful.

4. The Inclination to Know the Truth

The inclination to truth is proper to spiritual nature. It is the source of communion between beings gifted with reason. It surfaces in the primary light that contains the first principles of speculative and practical reason, especially in the moral principle that "good is to be done and evil avoided." It engenders love of the truth, analogous to every creature's yearning for the light.

From these first perceptions of the intellect, through the work of reason and in the encounter with reality, the different sciences are derived, especially moral science. Moral science considers all things from the perspective of the good, taking as its rules the precepts of the natural law. The task of this science is to apply these precepts judiciously and effectively in concrete actions, seeking to assure their excellence and perfection.

Different virtues perfect the intellect for this labor, which greatly depends on experience: There is *science*, understood as the capacity to study and direct one's actions, and also *wisdom*, which draws together knowledge and experience into a unified view of life and action. More specifically there is *prudence*, which discerns the good of an individual act. Prudence is the virtue of reason that enters into the action to fashion it. In moralities of virtue, prudence has a central function, corresponding to the role of conscience in moralities of obligation. There is this difference, however: Prudence seeks to discover what is best in the concrete, and not merely what is permitted or forbidden.

Its action is twofold: the practical judgment and the injunction to act, which moves one to act. One is not truly prudent if one does not effect the action.

The natural inclination to the truth is universal in its scope. Yet it acquires a particular focus in the moral life when joined to one's active experience, where all of reality is reflected as in a microcosm, especially through one's existential relations with others and with God. The inclination to the truth is the concern of the eighth commandment, which forbids false promises and lying. These negative precepts are at the service of a dynamic yearning that establishes different rights and duties: the right to an education according to the relative means of one's society and one's individual capacity; the subsequent duty to cultivate one's mind, especially in the moral domain, as it touches on one's own life situation and concrete problems. The intellect has a primary function to fulfill in the moral life. This function needs to be restored, especially in its contemplative dimension.

The yearning for truth provides a natural foundation for the Christian faith because faith is more than a voluntary obedience. It responds to the light of the revealing Word through an intellectual acceptance, as occurs between a master and his disciple. Faith develops love of truth with the aid of the gifts of knowledge and understanding. Because of the love that accompanies it, faith instills in us a certain connaturality with divine realities. It enlightens and nourishes our spiritual experience.

5. The Natural Inclination to Life in Society

The inclination to life in society presupposes a specific conception of the human person as a "social" or "political animal," as a being spontaneously drawn to associate with others. Without doubt this tendency rests on our need of others for survival, but it has a deeper foundation: the awareness of the other that dawns in love, affection, and friendship, and is destroyed by the opposite sentiments. Mutual friendship is more natural than struggle and rivalry. Man is not primarily a wolf to man, although he can become one.

The sign of this natural disposition is language. In contrast to animals that merely exchange cries, humans have invented a language that enables them to communicate their thoughts, feelings, and needs, to express good and evil, justice and injustice, to reveal the inner movements of their mind and heart. The whole life of the human person can be transcribed in language. The natural inclinations, in particular, are reflected in the very grammatical structure of language. The understanding of the good is expressed in qualifiers; the awareness of being in nouns; sexuality is expressed in words having gender; truth is displayed in the verb that determines the true and the false; lastly, the inclination to life in society is found in the pronouns, "I," "you," "he," and in singular and plural names. We can even establish a relationship between the inclinations and the senses, according to a certain affinity between them. We can associate the good with taste, with the savor (*sapor*) that gave its name to wisdom (*sapientia*). Sight is the most cognitive of the senses and is related to truth.

Language is linked to hearing. Touch and smell put us in contact with what is; they also play a role in sexuality. These are only suggestive signs, but they are revelatory of the natural character of our inclinations.

The primitive character of the inclination to life in society has great consequences for our conception of the human person. According to the theory of the freedom of indifference, the individual is primary: He stands in isolation from others and asserts his freedom. The struggle to satisfy one's needs, sets humans in opposition to each other, and provokes a rivalry that endangers the lives of all. Struggle is primary here. Society will be viewed as an artificial creation resting on the power delegated by the collectivity of individuals to a supreme authority – a king or a state – so that it can impose and maintain the peace, which is indispensable to all.

On the other hand, according to the freedom for excellence, because of the inclination that draws people together, society is natural to the human person. This inclination manifests itself as a spontaneous love or friendship that takes different forms according to the various types of communication: familial affection, personal friendship, natural feeling, social solidarity, or the solidarity of those in the same trade, and so forth. The assistance provided by society, beginning with the work of educators, is necessary for the formation and maturation of freedom. The inevitable struggles that arise between people, no matter how fierce they may be, are always grafted onto the natural desire for friendship, like a fever or a wound that enters the body it afflicts.

The inclination to life in society is developed by the virtue of justice, understood as the firm will to give to each one what is due to him. The object of justice is right, in its objective sense, expressed by the law. Justice covers exterior interactions with others on the familial, social, and national levels, but it also exists in relation to God in the virtue of religion. Justice, therefore, has a universal range. Its rule establishes either a strict or a relative equality in exchanges. Its goal is harmony and peace. Beyond justice there is friendship, as the flowering of human relations into a more personal relationship of reciprocal benevolence in freedom and equality.

On the Christian plane, we once again encounter charity as the virtue that inspires these relationships at the heart of the Church, a society that is simultaneously spiritual and institutional. We should note once again how this differs from other conceptions of the Church. Freedom of indifference fosters rivalry between powers, opposition between the freedom of individuals and of institutions, and so forth. Freedom for excellence seeks above all coordination and collaboration, and the development of the Church as a harmonious body.

To the degree that this is possible, we have shown how the natural law is not externally imposed on the human person by some foreign reality or will. It is truly interior. It is present from birth. It is inscribed on our hearts by the hand of God, who has fashioned us in his image. We can, no doubt, engrave these precepts in stone or write them in books, but they coincide with the yearnings that nourish the dynamism of our faculties. Thus, it is not a static law, even if its prescriptions contain restrictive formulations. It is essentially dynamic, like the virtues that it has the task of shaping within us.

The Role of the Natural Law in the Stages of Moral Education

It will be helpful to consider how the role of law varies according to the stages of moral education that guide the growth of freedom. In the first stage, dedicated to the apprenticeship of learning rules and self-discipline, we experience law as something external. Concretely, law is presented to us by our teachers. Its primary task is to combat in us the defects, sins, and harmful outgrowths of wishes and desires. At this stage, a certain constraint in the form of obligation is necessary in order to solidify the foundations of the moral life. This constraint is expressed in the negative precepts of the Ten Commandments. The art of the educator will be to help the pupil perceive the correspondence between these obligations and one's deepest yearnings for truth and goodness.

It is at this level that moralities of obligation retain their value. Historically, they fulfilled for centuries the role of offering the Christian people their first moral education. The reproach that we can make of them is that they limited the moral life to the domain of obligations and to the struggle against sin. They failed to show sufficiently that the deep law of the moral life, at the root of all obligations, is the tendency and yearning for progress, something that is true for all forms of life; nor did they understand how to prepare the faithful for the later stages of moral growth.

This critique, however, is not directed at the role of obligation as such, for obligation is indispensable at this stage of moral development. Indeed, it would be a grave illusion to attempt to construct a morality without obligations. The task of the moralist is to indicate the exact role of obligation in the service of the virtues that guide moral development. Obligation is there to teach the rudiments, the essential precepts, and to delineate those things without which virtue is not possible, without which moral development is not possible. Thus, murder is forbidden because it destroys justice and charity.

The second stage of moral progress, characterized by one's growing personal initiative, entails an interiorization of the law, resulting from an ever-increasing awareness of the correspondence between these precepts and our best and most intimate aspirations. This arises from the experience of right action. One becomes inclined to follow the law, not from constraint but from attraction and one's own preference, in spite of the weaknesses and contrary inclinations that can still remain within us. One discovers that virtue produces joy, beyond the level of one's efforts and trials.

At the third stage of moral development, the stage of maturity and mastery, the law becomes the support of an inventive and creative power within us, the instrument of the Spirit who infuses into our acts their full moral and spiritual excellence. We begin to understand why St. Thomas called the grace of the Holy Spirit a law: This grace, by means of charity, inspires the moral progress of the believer and leads it to an ever-deeper perfection. Law, therefore, is associated with the interior unfolding of wisdom and goodness. It marks its rhythm.

The natural law is indelibly inscribed on the human heart. This does not mean that we cannot transgress it, or even deny it through certain theories or ways of life: Yet the natural law always reasserts itself in the yearning for truth and goodness, and in the awareness of the other, that form the interlaced lines of a single attraction for moral excellence. No lie, no crime, no errant wanderings can destroy nor truly efface this primitive law. No matter how long the detour, the natural law always comes back to us one way or another.

This law is also universal, like reason itself. The law illumines reason and secretly directs its work, permeating cultural forms and systems of ideas, inspiring their variety and evolution. It offers to all people a common foundation and basic criteria of moral appreciation. Understood in this way, the natural law can solidly found and sustain the doctrine of human rights, beyond distinctions between nations and races, times and cultures. It is supple enough to adapt to inevitable differences and strong enough to inspire renewals and convergences. This feature is crucial to moral theology, for moral theology must inspire progress if it truly wishes once again to become a science of life and action.

Conclusion

A Vigilant Moral Theology

> Gird your loins and keep your lamps lit, and be
> like servants who await their master's return
> from a wedding, ready to open immediately
> when he comes and knocks (*Lk* 12.35–36).

Like a vigilant servant, Catholic moral theology has carefully kept its lamp lit ever since the Lord entrusted it with the flame of the Gospel. This light, maintained with fervor, brilliantly illumined the Roman basilicas through the preaching of the Fathers and the celebration of the liturgy. After being collected under strong Romanesque vaults, moral theology stretched further heavenward with the supple grace of gothic columns, supported by the harmonious order of the virtues. Regrouped around the Ten Commandments by the Council of Trent, it was given a chair in the seminaries and sat in the confessionals of baroque churches.

The Second Vatican Council took the lamp of moral theology in hand and exposed it to the winds of the open air so that its light might radiate more broadly throughout the world. Notice, however, that its flame wavers and bends back to earth. Where will we find the oil to return the flame to its former vigor? Will we understand that there is only one good merchant on this earth, the Holy Spirit, and only one treasure of sufficient value, the coin of faith marked with the seal of Jesus, son of Mary and son of God? In him, the Master, the hidden spark resides. In him is found the living seed that germinates anew in the hearts of the most humble as well as in the great assembly of the Church, before all the peoples. Through him, may the light of our lamps shine unfailingly in eyes full of hope and in lives full of love.

Lexicon

agape: a Greek term employed in the New Testament to signify the love of Christ, fraternal love, charity, and spiritual love.

casuistry: moral analysis centered on the study of cases of conscience.

catechesis: religious instruction following Baptism, hence the term "catechism."

charism: gifts of the Holy Spirit for the service of the Church.

charity: a love that comes from God through Christ and is infused by the Holy Spirit. It is the principal virtue. Its effects include joy, peace, mercy, and beneficence.

ethics: morality understood from the philosophical perspective; the study of the criteria of judgment concerning action.

magisterium: authority in the Church entrusted with teaching and regulating faith and morals.

nominalism: a system of thought that affirms that nothing is real except the individual and his singular acts. Universal concepts have only a "nominal" value. It focuses morality on the relationship between free acts and legal obligation.

norm: law understood as a rational regulation.

paraclesis: an urgent moral exhortation, embracing the Commandments and the virtues and directed toward the perfection of charity.

parenesis: spiritual exhortation liberally joined to moral imperatives.

proportionalism: a system that judges acts by the balance or proportion between the good and evil consequences they produce. It is also called "consequentialism."

virtue: a quality of heart and mind, of reason and will, that disposes a person to engage in acts and works of excellence, perfect in their composition.

Selected Bibliography

Aquinas, Thomas. *Summa Theologica*. Translated by the Fathers of the English Dominican Province. New York: Benziger Brothers, 1947.

_____. *Summa Contra Gentiles*. 5 Volumes. Notre Dame, Ind.: University of Notre Dame Press, 1975.

Augustine. *The Catholic and Manichaean Ways of Life*. (*De moribus ecclesiae catholicae et de moribus manichaeorum*) Translated by Donald A. Gallagher and Idella J. Gallagher. Washington, D.C.: Catholic University of America Press, 1966.

_____. *The Lord's Sermon on the Mount*. Translated by John J. Jepson. Westminster, Md.: Newman Press, 1948.

_____. *On Christian Doctrine*. Translated by D. W. Robertson. New York: Macmillan, 1958.

Bouyer, Louis. *History of Christian Spirituality*. Translated by Mary P. Ryan. New York: Desclée, 1963.

Catholic Church. *Catechism of the Catholic Church*. Mahwah, N.J.: Paulist Press, 1994.

Cerfaux, Lucien. *Christ in the Theology of St. Paul*. Translated by Geoffrey Webb. New York: Herder, 1959.

Cessario, Romanus. *Christian Faith and the Theological Life*. Washington, D.C.: Catholic University of America Press, 1996.

_____. *The Moral Virtues and Theological Ethics.* Notre Dame, Ind.: University of Notre Dame Press, 1991.

Chenu, Marie-Dominique. *Toward Understanding St. Thomas.* Translated by A. M. Landry and D. Hughes. Chicago: Regnery, 1964.

Curran, Charles E. *The Origins of Moral Theology in the United States: Three Different Approaches.* Washington, D.C.: Georgetown University Press, 1997.

Deman, Thomas. *Aux Origines de la Théologie Morale.* Conférence Albert-le-Grand. Paris: Librairie J. Vrin, 1951.

_____. "Probabilisme." In *Dictionnaire de théologie catholique.* Volume 13. Paris: Letouzey et Ané, 1936.

Delhaye, Philip. *Le Décalogue et sa place dans la morale chrétienne.* Paris: La Pensée Catholique, 1963.

_____. *The Christian Conscience.* Translated by Charles Underhill Quinn. New York: Desclée, 1968.

Finnis, John. *Fundamentals of Ethics.* Washington, D.C.: Georgetown University Press, 1983.

Gregory of Nyssa. *The Beatitudes.* Translated by Hilda C. Graef. Westminster, Md.: Newman Press, 1954.

Grisez, Germain. *The Way of the Lord Jesus.* Volume 1: *Christian Moral Principles.* Chicago: Franciscan Herald Press, 1983.

Häring, Bernard. *The Law of Christ.* Translated by Edwin G. Kaiser. Paramus, N.J.: Newman Press, 1961.

Jone, Heribert. *Moral Theology.* Translated by Urban Adelman. Westminster, Md.: Newman Press, 1963.

Jonsen, Albert R., and Toulmin, Stephen. *The Abuse of Casuistry*. Berkeley: University of California Press, 1988.

Lagarde, Georges de. *La Naissance de l'esprit laïque au déclin du Moyen Age*. Louvain: E. Nauwelaerts, 1946.

Lottin, Odon. *Morale Fondamentale*. Tournai, Belgium: Desclée, 1954.

Lyonnet, Stanislaus, and Potterie, Ignace de la. *The Christian Lives by the Spirit*. Preface by Yves Congar. Translated by John Morriss. Staten Island, N.Y.: Alba House, 1971.

McInerny, Ralph. *Ethica Thomistica: The Moral Philosophy of Thomas Aquinas*. Washington, D.C.: Catholic University of America Press, 1982.

MacIntyre, Alasdair. *Three Rival Versions of Moral Enquiry*. Notre Dame. Ind.: University of Notre Dame Press, 1990.

MacNamara, Vincent. *Faith and Ethics: Recent Roman Catholicism*. Washington, D.C.: Georgetown University Press, 1985.

Mahoney, John. *The Making of Moral Theology: A Study of the Roman Catholic Tradition*. Oxford: Clarendon Press, 1987.

Mehl, Roger. *Catholic Ethics and Protestant Ethics*. Translated by James H. Farley. Philadelphia: Westminster Press, 1971.

Meilaender, Gilbert C. *The Theory and Practice of Virtue*. Notre Dame, Ind.: University of Notre Dame Press, 1984.

O'Donovan, Oliver. *Resurrection and Moral Order: an Outline for Evangelical Ethics*. Grand Rapids, Mich.: Eerdmans, 1986.

O'Meara, Thomas F. *Thomas Aquinas Theologian*. Notre Dame, Ind.: University of Notre Dame Press, 1997.

Pieper, Josef. Faith, *Hope and Love.* San Francisco: Ignatius Press, 1997.

_____. *The Four Cardinal Virtues.* Edition with Notes. Notre Dame, Ind.: University of Notre Dame Press, 1966.

Pinckaers, Servais. *The Pursuit of Happiness – God's Way: Living the Beatitudes.* New York: Alba House, 1998.

_____. *Le Renouveau de la Morale.* Preface by M. D. Chenu. Paris: Téqui, 1964.

_____. *The Sources of Christian Ethics.* Translated by Mary Thomas Noble. Washington, D.C.: Catholic University of America Press, 1995.

_____. *La Vie selon l'Esprit: Essai de théologie spirituelle selon saint Paul et saint Thomas d'Aquin.* In Amateca, *Manuels de théologie catholique.* Volume 17.2 Luxembourg: Editions Saint Paul, 1996.

Porter, Jean. *The Recovery of Virtue: The Relevance of Aquinas for Christian Ethics.* Louisville, Ky.: Westminster/John Knox Press, 1990.

Prat, Ferdinand. *The Theology of St. Paul.* Translated by John L. Stoddard. Westminster, Md.: Newman Bookshop, 1952.

Prümmer, Dominic. *Handbook of Moral Theology.* Translated by Gerald W. Shelton. New York: P. J. Kennedy, 1957.

Regamey, Pie-Raymond. *Portrait spirituel du chrétien.* Paris: Éditions du Cerf, 1963.

Rhonheimer, Martin. *Natural Law and Practical Reason: A Thomist View of Moral Autonomy.* Translated by Gerald Malsbary. New York: Fordham University Press, 2000.

_____. *Praktische Vernunft und Vernunftigkeit der Praxis: Handlungstheorie bei Thomas von Aquin in ihrer Entstehung aus dem Problemkontext der aristotelischen Ethik.* Berlin: Akademie Verlag, 1994.

Schnackenburg, Rudolf. *The Moral Teaching of the New Testament.* Translated by J. Holland Smith and W. S. O'Hara. New York: Herder, 1967.

Schneewind, J. B. *The Invention of Autonomy: A History of Modern Moral Philosophy.* Cambridge: Cambridge University Press, 1997.

Schockenhoff, Eberhard. *Bonum Hominis: Die Anthropologischen und Theologischen Grundlagen der Tugendethik des Thomas Von Aquin.* Mainz: Matthias-Grünewald-Verlag, 1987.

Spicq, Ceslas. *Agapé in the New Testament.* Three Volumes. Translated by Marie Aquinas McNamara and Mary Honoria Richter. St. Louis: Herder, 1966.

_____. *Connaissance et morale dans la Bible.* Fribourg, Switzerland: Éditions Universitaires, 1985.

_____. *Theological Lexicon of the New Testament.* Three Volumes. Peabody, Mass.: Hendrickson, 1994.

_____. *Théologie morale du Nouveau Testament.* Two Volumes. Paris: Librairie Lecoffre, 1965.

Taylor, Charles. *The Ethics of Authenticity.* Cambridge, Mass.: Harvard University Press, 1991.

Torrell, Jean-Pierre. *Saint Thomas Aquinas. Volume 1: The Person and his Work.* Translated by Robert Royal. Washington, D.C.: Catholic University of America Press, 1996.

_____. *Saint Thomas d'Aquin: Maître Spirituel: Initiation 2.* Paris: Éditions du Cerf, 1996.

Weisheipl, James. *Friar Thomas D'Aquino: His Life, Thought, and Work.* New York: Doubleday, 1974.

Westberg, Daniel. *Right Practical Reason: Aristotle, Action, and Prudence in Aquinas.* Oxford: Clarendon Press, 1994.

Woods, Walter J. *Walking with Faith: New Perspectives on the Sources and Shaping of Catholic Moral Life.* Collegeville, Minn.: Michael Glazier Press, 1998.

Index of Names

Index of Subjects

Action, 10, 16, 27, 46, 51–52, 61, 68–69, 76, 82, 87, 89, 93, 97, 105, 110–11; and freedom, 23, 27, 29, 49, 68, 70–71, 74; and grace, 28, 49; and joy, 70, 78; and law, 34, 36, 56, 70,72; and love, 88, 102; and natural inclination, 98, 102; and reason, 73; and the virtues, 70, 88, 102; in St. Thomas Aquinas, 26–29; in the Revisionists, 53–54; judgment of, 52–58, 105–6, 114; of the Church, 93; of the Holy Spirit, 16, 71, 81–83, 92–93; principles of, 26, 28; ultimate end of, 27, 66, 74. See also act(s)

act(s) 10, 27, 29, 33, 35, 49, 52, 54–56, 59–60, 65–66, 68–69, 71–74, 78, 82, 88, 89, 101, 104–5, 111, 114–15; and law, 34, 56; intrinsically evil act(s), 52–53, 61; of faith, 12, 86; principles of, 27–29; voluntary act(s), 27. *See also* action

agape, 13, 114

apprenticeship, 70, 109

arts, 55, 69–70, 82, 86

autonomy, vii, 48–50, 61

Baptism, 82, 92, 114

beatitude. See happiness

Beatitudes, 8–9, 60, 78, 92; in St. Augustine, 22; in St. Thomas Aquinas, 22, 27, 29; in the Fathers of the Church, 9, 67

body 12; analogy of, 87, 92, 108; in St. Paul, 12–13, 15, 86; of Christ, 13, 15, 86, 93

cases of conscience 46–47, 49, 55, 74, 114; and the natural law, 53; in the manuals, 33–34, 36, 38–39, 56, 73; in St. Paul, 14–15, 17

casuistry, 34, 50, 74, 114

catechesis, 2, 7–8, 11, 101, 114

categorical imperative, 66, 73

charism, 15, 28–29, 88, 114

charity, 14, 35, 44, 67, 90, 92, 94–95, 110, 114–15; and Christ, 20, 88; and friendship with God, 91; and happiness, 20–21, 67; and natural love, 102; and the gifts,

126

Scriptural Index
(bold numbers refer to pages)